Kali Thea

bells

by **Yasmin Whittaker Khan**

First performed on
23 March 2005 at
Birmingham REP,
The Door

chaos

by **Azma Dar**

First performed on
16 March 2005 at
Birmingham REP,
The Door

kalí

CHAOS

By **Azma Dar**

Salim	Damian Asher
Babar	Marc Elliott
Mr Rizvi	Nicholas Khan
Mrs Rizvi	Shelley King
Aunty Moona	Jamila Massey

Director	Janet Steel
Designer	Matthew Wright
Lighting	Chris Corner
Composer	Sayan Kent
Assistant Director	Sophie Austin
Dramaturgy	Penny Gold
Stage Manager	Sarah Pearce

Project Manager	Christopher Corner
Marketing Consultant	Suman Bhuchar
Press Representative	David Bloom
	for Guy Chapman Associates
Graphic Design	Luke Wakeman

First performance: 16 March 2005 at Birmingham Rep, The Door

Kali would like to thank the Directors and everyone at Birmingham Rep for all their help and support with presenting *Chaos*.

Thanks to Richard Lee at The Jerwood Space, Dawn Garrigan at Arts Council England, Ben Payne at Birmingham Rep, Sarah Tibbatts, Binita Walia, Marilyn Kingwell, everyone at Southwark Playhouse, Dan at Hedgehog, Carly Ramsay, Hasbro, Sommerfields and those whose help came too late to be mentioned here.

Subsidised rehearsal space provided by JERWOOD SPACE

Chaos

I began writing Chaos a few months after September 11th when the terrorist attacks in New York had left the whole world in a state of shock and confusion. Although most of us, thankfully, didn't have to endure the terrible pain suffered by the victims and their families, it seemed to me that many people were affected in some way or other, even if it was only that they were questioning the beliefs, ideals, and truths in their lives.

All the Muslims I knew condemned the killings, but when the war against Afghanistan and further violence against innocent people followed (this time it was 'unintentional'), I began to see how some people might find their loyalties drifting. With all the conspiracy theories, censored news reports, confessional video diaries, and leaders of all kinds bombarding us with their own ideas, much of the time people didn't know what to think or who to believe.

I was also thinking about families, and about secrets, resentments and unspoken things that simmer beneath the fabric of most homes, and how they cause splits and divisions in relationships.

In *Chaos*, I've tried to explore some wider social and political concerns through the conflicts and dilemmas of the Rizvi family. When each member takes a different stance on big global issues and becomes lost in their own world, the family begins to crack and gradually, deeper, more personal troubles are revealed.

In the end, I think the play is about the dangers of obsession and extremism of any kind, the need for tolerance and understanding, and what happens when people stop listening to each other.

Azma Dar, 2005

kalí
BELLS

By **Yasmin Whittaker Khan**

Charles	Damian Asher
Pepsi	Marc Elliott
Aiesha	Shivan Ghai
Ashraf	Nicholas Khan
Madam	Sharona Sassoon

Director	Poonam Brah
Designer	Matthew Wright
Lighting	Chris Corner
Composer	Sayan Kent
Choroegraphy	Kella Panay
Assistant Director	Pia Furtado
Dramaturgy	Penny Gold
Stage Manager	Sarah Pearce

Project Manager	Christopher Corner
Marketing Consultant	Suman Bhuchar
Press Representative	David Bloom
	for Guy Chapman Associates
Graphic Design	Luke Wakeman

First performance: 23 March 2005 at Birmingham Rep, The Door

Kali would like to thank the Directors and everyone at Birmingham Rep for all their help and support with presenting *Bells*.

Thanks to Richard Lee at The Jerwood Space, Dawn Garrigan at Arts Council England, Ben Payne at Birmingham Rep, Sarah Tibbatts, Binita Walia, Marilyn Kingwell, everyone at Southwark Playhouse, Dan at Hedgehog, Mark Pann, Carly Ramsay and those whose help came too late to be mentioned here.

Subsidised rehearsal space provided by JERWOOD SPACE

Bells

Bells is a fiction based on my research into Mujra clubs in the UK. I've been fascinated since seeing them portrayed in films as a child. Then I aspired to the pretty clothes, the dancing prowess and apparent natural grace of the courtesans. Now I have the glittery clothes but little dancing grace – and I'm still fascinated.

The love, support and sense of justice I've had from my family, especially my Mum and Dad, has given me the strength to write about the many issues that pique my interest or make me laugh even if they are difficult.

I'm fascinated how overtly the Mujra culture is displayed in Bollywood/Lollywood films and music, yet I've not come across any serious concern about the reality of Mujra clubs. It's rumoured that Lollywood has worked with actresses from the Heera Mandi area of Lahore and Mujra dancers strive to be scouted. The films glamorise life in these clubs and so families gather to watch the latest blockbuster.

My research has left me sickened by the hypocrisy, psychological bullying, use of money as power and the seediness of these clubs. Some *respectable*, even *religious* men visit Mujra clubs – condemning these vulnerable women in public whilst pursuing them in private. Beneath the exploitation and degradation of the unprotected and sometimes helpless, there are many lonely and pained individuals – both buying and selling the entertainment.

A special thank you to Penny Gold and Micheline Steinberg Associates for all their support and encouragement.

Yasmin Whittaker Khan, 2005

kali

Kali seeks out strong individual Asian women writers who challenge our perceptions through original and thought-provoking theatre. The company has established a reputation for presenting work that takes audiences on unpredictable journeys that entertain, excite and inspire.

Calcutta Kosher 2003

Since its inception in 1990, Kali's connections within the Asian community have made it a natural home for women who are seeking new ways to express and explore the issues and human interest stories of the Diaspora.

Sock 'em With Honey 2003

Kali aims to present the distinct perspective and experience of Asian women to people from all backgrounds and to celebrate that richness and diversity.

kali

No idea is too small, no statement too large. We actively encourage our writers and audience to reinvent and reshape the theatrical agenda.

Through our *Kali Shorts* and *Kali Futures* programmes, we provide core resources for writers new to the theatre through workshops, dramaturgical support and public readings.

Singh Tangos 2002

River On Fire 2000

Artistic Director:
Janet Steel

Board of Trustees:
Helena Bell
Penny Gold
Shyama Perera
Shiroma Silva
Jocelyn Watson
Rita Wolf
Kamila Zahno

Kali Theatre Co.
Colombo Centre,
34-68 Colombo Street,
London, SE1 6DP
Ltd Co. No. 2583595

020 7021 0000
info@kalitheatre.co.uk
www.kalitheatre.co.uk
Registered Charity No. 1071733

Cast in alphabetical order

DAMIAN ASHER Salim (*Chaos*) / Charles (*Bells*)

Damian Trained at Guildford School of Acting. Theatre includes: *Monkey in the Stars* (Polka), *The Phoenix and the Carpet*, (Chester Gateway), *East Is East* (Leicester Haymarket), *Dealers Choice* (Salisbury Playhouse), *My Dad's Cornershop* (Derby Playhouse), The Maids (Naach Theatre at Lyric Hammersmith). TV includes: *The Bill, Hetty Wainthrop Investigates, Doctors, Being April, Strange, According to Bex*. Film includes: *Bollywood Queen, Cool Blokes: Decent Suits, Naked In London*.

MARC ELLIOT Babar (*Chaos*) / Pepsi (*Bells*)

Marc made his professional debut with the RSC in *Julius Caesar. Later he* was in *A Winters Tale, Macbeth* and the premiere of Nigel Williams' *Lord of the Flies* (The Other Place). Theatre includes: *Two Lost Souls On A Dirty Night* (Latchmere), *The Mill On The Floss* (Loft Theatre), *Romeo and Juliet* (Tour), *Les Liasions Dangereuses* (Vienna English Theatre), *Mandragora, King of India* (Tara Arts tour). He played Jean in *Miss Julie* and Claire in *The Maids* for Naach Theatre (Lyric Hammersmith). Radio includes: *The Mob, Jadoo, The 10th Man*. Marc made his TV debut this year in *Mile High*.

SHIVANI GHAI Aiesha (*Bells*)

Originally from Newcastle, Shivani studied drama at the Birmingham Theatre School before moving to London. Theatre credits include: *Cornershop* (Man Mela), *Bollywood 2000* (The Reduced Indian Film Company), *Made in India* (Hungama), *Bollywood Yet Another Love Story* (RIFCO), *Can U Kick it* (Caught In The Act), *Made In England* (Firebrand). Film and TV credits include: *Doctors* (BBC), *The Bill* (Granada), *Spooks,* (KUDOS), *My Hero,* (BBC), *Adventures Inc* (GTV), *Day Of The Sirens* (Imaginary Films), *Bride and Prejudice* (Bride Productions), *The Camping Trip* (Frigid Films/BBC), *Red Mercury* (Dirty Bomb Films). Radio:*There Comes a Khama* (BBC).

NICHOLAS KHAN Mr Rizvi (*Chaos*) / Ashraf (*Bells*)

Theatre includes: *Who's Afraid of the Big Bad Book* (Soho Theatre), *Passage To India* (Shared Experience), *Messiah* (Directed by Steven Berkoff), *The Lion, The Witch and The Wardrobe, Winters Tale, Comedy of Errors, Romeo and Juliet, Henry V* (RSC), *Mincemeat* (Cardboard Citizens), *Arabian Nights* (Young Vic), *Animal Crackers* (Manchester Royal Exchange), *Maa* (Royal Court), *Alice Through The Looking Glass, Punchkin, The Wonderland Adventures of Alice, Ali Baba, Aladdin, Dick Whittington* (London Bubble). TV includes: *Casualty, East Enders, The Genius of Mozart, Holby City, Gory Greek Gods* (BBC).

SHELLEY KING Mrs Rizvi (*Chaos*)

Theatre includes: *Bombay Dreams* (Really Useful Theatre Co), *Besharam* (Soho Theatre/ Birmingham Rep), *River on Fire* (Kali), *Orpheus, The Modern Husband, Ion* (Actors Touring Company), *Women of Troy, Tartuffe, Little Clay Cart* (RNT), *Heer Ranjha, Antigone, Danton's Death* (Tara Arts), *The Crutch* (Royal Court), *Death and the Maiden* (Wolsey, Ipswich), *Damon and Pythias* (Globe), *Top Girls* (Royal Northampton), *Hobson's Choice* (Young Vic), *Calcutta Kosher* (Kali Theatre), *Behtzi* (Birmingham Rep). TV includes *Silent Witness* (BBC), *See How They Run* (BBC/ ABC), *Angels* (BBC), *Tandoori Nights* (Channel 4). Film Includes: *Code 46* (BBC/Revolution Films).

JAMILA MASSEY Aunty Moona (*Chaos*)

Born in Simla and came to England at age 12, later graduating from Kings College London. Theatre includes: *The Great Celestial Cow* (Royal Court), *Conduct Unbecoming* (Canada & UK tour), *Song for a Sanctuary* (Kali Theatre/Lyric Hammersmith), *Women of the Dust* (Tamasha/Bristol Old Vic), *The Life & Loves of Mr Patel* (Leicester Haymarket), *Moti Roti Puttli Chunni* (Theatre Royal Stratford East & international tour), Calcutta Kosher (Kali Theatre). TV includes: *The Jewel In The Crown*, 33 episodes of *Mind Your Language, All About Me, Doctors, Albion Market, Langley Bottom, Churchill's People, Pie In The Sky, Casualty, Coronation Street Arabian*

Nights, Perfect World, Family Pride, Eastenders. Film includes: *Madame Sousatzka, King of Bollywood, Wild West, Chicken Tikka Masala*. Radio: *Auntie Satya* in *The Archers*. A regular broadcaster for BBC Home and World Services. With her husband, Reginald Massey, she has written books on the music and dance of India.

SHARONA SASSOON Madam (*Bells*)

Sharona started acting at the Finch Stage School and went onto further study with a BA in Performing Arts. Her final year of study was spent in America at New Paltz State University New York. Sharona's big stage debut came with *Bombay Dreams* in which she was the female swing as well as understudying the role of Kitty. Other theatre credits include *Blood on the Pavement* at the Cockpit Theatre and playing Mabel in *Fame* at the Gordon Craig Theatre. Sharona is delighted to be working with the Kali Theatre in such a challenging role.

Company

AZMA DAR Writer (*Chaos*)

Azma Dar was born in Ashford and grew up in Pinner. She studied art at Central Saint Martins College and then completed a degree in Literature and Classical Studies. Shortly afterwards she joined the Young Writers' Programme at the Royal Court, and began writing plays and a novel. Her work is usually inspired by the people she meets, the odd stories they have to tell and the darkness, hope, and absurdity of the human spirit. She is currently developing a new work with Theatre Royal Stratford East and Watermans Arts Centre. *Chaos* is her first full-length play.

YASMIN WHITTAKER KHAN Writer (*Bells*)

Recent work includes: *Love Stomp* (with Kadam Dance Co); *Pleasure and Pain* and *Lucy* (Menagerie Theatre Co). Yasmin is developing a new play for Theatre Royal Stratford East about Asian women who've been incarcerated in the UK, and is also under commission to M6 Theatre Company. Film: *Lemon Juke Box* (a five minute short). This year she developed *Le Grand Jour*, a short film produced in association with Revolution Films for refugee week. TV: Yasmin co-presented, researched and scripted a series for Anglia TV (With Paul Ross). Radio: BBC Radio Asian Network's *Silver Street*.

JANET STEEL Director (*Chaos*)

Artistic Director of Kali, with an MA in Theatre Practice, Janet began her career as an actress. Theatre: *Cinders*, *A Colder Climate* (Royal Court), *Blood Wedding* (Half Moon), *Romeo and Juliet* (Sherman Theatre & Albany Empire), *Oedipus Rex* (Tara Arts). **TV:** *An English Christmas*, *The Bride, Gems, The Refuge, Shalom Salaam*. Janet began directing as assistant to Tessa Schneideman at Loose Change Theatre, producing UK premiers at BAC by Spanish authors, where she directed her first full-length piece, *White Biting Dog*. Directing: *April in Paris, Bretevski Street, A Hard Rain, Top Girls* (Northampton Royal Theatre), *Exodus* (Millennium Mysteries at Coventry Belgrade), Brecht's *Antigone, The Mother*, *Orpheus Descending, An Ideal Husband, Romeo & Juliet, The Knockey, Serious Money* (Rose Bruford College). For Kali: *Sock 'em with Honey* and *Calcutta Kosher*. Last December Janet directed *Behzti* at Birmingham Rep.

POONAM BRAH Director (*Bells*)

Theatre as Director includes: *Lady with a Lapdog* (Experimental work, Young Vic Studio), Staged readings of *Chess, King Saturn* and *Bells* (Stratford East, Soho Theatre, Birmingham Rep, Oldham Coliseum), *Unfinished Business* (White Bear), *Girl Talk/Sami* (New Experimental Theatre, Mumbai), *Reader I Murdered Him, Black Tigers, Invisible, The I of the Needle* (King's Head), *Andorra, The Bacchae* (Warwick Arts Centre). As Assistant Director: *Calcutta Kosher* (Stratford East), *Skellig* (Young Vic), *Hobson's Choice* (Young Vic and Tour), *Sock 'em with Honey* (Kali Theatre and Tour), *Bless the Bride, Billy Liar; Lebensraum, The Vagina Monologues* (King's Head).

MATTHEW WRIGHT Designer

Matthew recently designed *Behzti* at Birmingham Rep for Janet Steel. Other recent work includes: *Clouds* (No. 1 Tour), *US And Them* and *The Dead Eye Boy* (Hampstead Theatre), *The Green Man* (Bush Theatre & Plymouth Theatre Royal), *Larkin With Women* (West Yorkshire Playhouse), *Arcadia, Summer Lightning* (Northampton Theatre Royal), *Getting To The Foot Of The Mountain* (Birmingham Rep), *Charley's Aunt, Private Lives* (Exeter Northcott) and *Four Night In Knaresborough* (Stoke New Vic Theatre). He is also designing *On The Ceiling* by Nigel Planer (Birmingham Rep), *Dancing at Lughnasa* (Stoke New Vic Theatre) and *One Under* by Winsome Pinnock (Tricycle Theatre).

SOPHIE AUSTIN Assistant Director (*Chaos*)

Sophie graduated from the Rose Bruford College Directing Course last year. Her London directorial debut was *Oedipus the King* at the Tristan Bates Theatre. Her assistant directing credits include *Dead Hands* written and directed by Howard Barker (Riverside Studios and national tour) and *The Life of Galileo* directed by David Salter and (Battersea Arts Centre). Sophie is also Artistic Director for Teatro Vivo, a South East London theatre collective.

PIA FURTADO Assistant Director (*Bells*)

Pia has performed in venues ranging from The Underbelly, Edinburgh to The Royal Albert Hall. Directing credits include *A Child Can Change The World* (Nehru Centre), *Yard Gal* (Garage Theatre), *All MY Sons* (Bloomsbury), *Leaving Home* (Kings Head). As assistant director projects include *A Girl In A Car With A Man* (Royal Court), *A Perfect Ganesh, Missing Marilyn* (Kings Head) and *Only You Can Save Mankind* (Pleasance).

CHAOS

BELLS

First published in 2005 by Oberon Books Ltd
521 Caledonian Road, London N7 9RH
Tel: 020 7607 3637 / Fax: 020 7607 3629
e-mail: oberon.books@btconnect.com
www.oberonbooks.com

A catalogue record for this book is available from the British
Library.

ISBN: 1 84002 554 9

Cover design by Luke Wakeman

Printed in Great Britain by Antony Rowe Ltd, Chippenham

Contents

CHAOS, 17

BELLS, 101

CHAOS

Characters

MR RIZVI

MRS RIZVI

SALIM

BABAR

AUNTY MOONA

SCENE 1

A living room. There is a dining table, spread with a smart new tablecloth. On it is a shiny silver candleholder, a vase of flowers, and a stack of plates. The rest of the furniture seems a little worn out in comparison to the polish and shine of the table and the objects on it. There are two sofas and a coffee table, a sideboard holding decorative items – maybe a silver cruet set, a fancy red and gold plastic tissue box holder, a teapot, a family photograph. The wall at the back is covered in striped wallpaper. There are framed Arabic surahs on the wall. There are two doors leading out – one to the kitchen and one to the main room (both offstage).

MRS RIZVI is reading namaaz [prayer], sitting. SALIM enters and begins arranging things on the table. She finishes (by looking over her right and left shoulders). She gets up and closes the door, then comes back to sit on the mat. She is reading something on her prayer beads. As she reads she is trying to see what SALIM is doing. She passes her hands over her face, gets up, folds the mat and puts it in the drawer of the sideboard. She takes out some incense sticks, lights them, and puts them on the table.

MRS RIZVI: There, that should add a nice, fragrant touch. It purifies the air. God knows this house needs cleansing.

She looks around distastefully.

I am relying on you to keep me informed, Salim.

SALIM: About what?

MRS RIZVI: On your father's movements this evening. You know I can't trust him.

SALIM: You'll be with him yourself, won't you?

MRS RIZVI: I've been with him for the last twenty-five years but it hasn't made any difference.

SALIM: Mum, you worry about nothing. Dad's not interested in anyone else.

MRS RIZVI: You haven't seen him in action. All that stroking and kissing.

SALIM: He has to be polite.

MRS RIZVI: But it's not right. Maybe I will give the mayor a cuddle tonight. We'll see how your father enjoys that.

SALIM hugs her.

SALIM: You've got me.

MRS RIZVI: Well yes, you're a good boy.

SALIM: Why don't you go and get ready?

MRS RIZVI: Maybe I won't go after all.

SALIM: Why not?

MRS RIZVI: All that noise, all those people. It's too much. I'd prefer to stay upstairs in peace and privacy. Anyway, what will I do there? It's not as if I'll be missed.

SALIM: Of course you'll be missed. Dad needs you by his side tonight. It's important to him.

MRS RIZVI: The party is important to him.

SALIM: Yes, and so are you.

MRS RIZVI: He never notices me when he's got other female company.

SALIM: He bought you a new suit.

MRS RIZVI: (*Cynical but with a tiny flicker of excitement.*) Did he?

SALIM: It was his idea.

MRS RIZVI: Oh, you mean he gave you some money and you bought it.

There are a couple of bags on the floor. She opens one and takes out a sparkly sleeveless kameez.

This? He wants me to parade around in a vest? Toba toba! And you, Saleem! I thought you had some sense of shame.

SALIM: No, no, Mum, that's not for you.

He tries to take it from her.

MRS RIZVI: Then whose is it? Who have you been buying ladies' garments for? Who is she?

SALIM: It's nothing like that, Mum.

MRS RIZVI: My God, it's not yours, is it?

SALIM: Mum! It's not mine. It's a present for…one of the guests.

MRS RIZVI: One of the guests? Which one? Tell me, Salim! I know he's up to no good. He told you to get it for her, didn't he? Then added me on as an afterthought.

SALIM: I got it for a colleague.

He takes the suit.

MRS RIZVI: You're lying.

SALIM: Honestly, he knows nothing about it. This one's for you.

He gives her the other bag and she takes the suit out to look at.

MRS RIZVI: You're a sensible boy. This is just my style. Your father doesn't understand fashion for the mature and respectable lady. He's more interested in younger models.

SALIM: Mum –

MRS RIZVI: You don't know, Salim, you don't know. Those late nights, that faraway look in his eyes, those unexpected fits of giggling – they can only mean one thing. The old fool thinks he's in love. I've seen it all once too, remember – in a time that's lost now. Before I was replaced by concepts and progressive thinking. The heart squeezed to quench the mind.

SALIM: You shouldn't think like that. Dad's just excited about the election. You know how hard he's been working. That's all it is. Now go and get ready.

MRS RIZVI: So naïve, my son.

She picks up the bags to go.

SALIM: You can leave that here.

MRS RIZVI: I'll put it upstairs for now and you can take it later. Otherwise your father will complain about stray shopping on the floor.

Exit MRS RIZVI. SALIM carries on arranging things. A few moments later MR RIZVI enters. He sniffs the air and looks around, trying to locate the source of the scent. He sees the incense and puts it out.

MR RIZVI: I suppose your mother did this. Trying to gas my guests.

He looks about, checking that she's not there, and then throws the incense in the bin. He examines the table, picking things up, rearranging.

MR RIZVI: I want everything to be perfect for tonight. Did you invite Mr Willoughby? MP Willoughby I mean.

SALIM: Yes, Dad, I told you last week.

MR RIZVI: And is he a confirmed arrival?

SAILM: So far, yes.

MR RIZVI: Good. And Mr Chadwin-Jones? Or C J, as I and his other close friends call him.

SALIM: He'll be here.

MR RIZVI: Good. Excellent. With the right people behind us – the world is our oyster, son. Think of the things we can achieve.

SALIM: Take things slowly, Dad.

Enter BABAR.

MR RIZVI: I know, I know. Deep breathing. Mustn't count my eggs.

BABAR: Chickens.

MR RIZVI: What?

BABAR: Chickens, not eggs. But don't put your eggs in one basket.

MR RIZVI is confused.

MR RIZVI: Pass over a simple mistake, can't you? I'm warning you – don't disgrace me tonight. Use this evening profitably. Do some networking, make some contacts. Is that the CV? Show me.

He grabs a paper from BABAR's hands.

Philosophy! Why couldn't you do something useful, like business or accounts? Look how well Salim's doing. He's been a real help to me. What will you do with philosophy? It's nothing but ideas.

BABAR: It stimulates me.

MR RIZVI: Will it stimulate you into finding you a good job? Make this CV more presentable. It's a very boring format. You've got access to modern technology – use it. Add some eye-catching graphics. Salim will help you.

He gives the paper back to SALIM. BABAR is annoyed.

SALIM: It looks okay – it's the conventional layout.

SALIM gives the paper to BABAR. He goes into the kitchen and returns with plates of food, covered with kitchen towel. One is covered with a dome-shaped net.

MR RIZVI: Exactly. You have to stand out from the crowd these days. Get noticed. Salim, put the dishes nicely on the table. A symmetrical arrangement is good. It gives the impression of order. Leave a few here and the rest can go inside. Where are the sausage rolls?

BABAR: You are living dangerously! Does Mum know?

MR RIZVI: I had them specially made from halaal sausages. Think of it! It shows how far we've progressed. When I arrived in this country the word sausage was like a swear-word for us. These are a symbol of my whole outlook – the union and mutual understanding of cultures.

BABAR: East and west meet within a flaky pastry.

MR RIZVI goes to the sideboard and opens the drawer. He takes out a poster tube and removes the lid.

MR RIZVI: (*To BABAR.*) You should have done politics. You would have been able to help me with my future campaigns. (*Pause.*) Councillor Jameel Rizvi. How does that sound? And later, who knows what letters might follow my name? And M and a P or even a P and an M. Oh, I'm just being silly.

He takes out the poster and unrolls it, holding it up. It is a campaign picture of him, smiling with his thumbs up. He admires it.

After what happened in New York, it's even more important for our voices to be heard. Maybe you should double-check once more Salim. Make sure everyone is still coming. I sent the invitations out some time ago – recent events might have put people off. I don't want to be entertaining an empty room.

SALIM: I've triple-checked everything, Dad.

MR RIZVI: Good boy. Those bastards have made life difficult for all of us.

He puts the poster on the table but it rolls up.

BABAR: Who, the FBI?

MR RIZVI is still unsuccessfully trying to put the poster flat on the table.

MR RIZVI: No, no, the…perpetrators of that…atrocity. Given us a bad name. You would do well to get rid of that cap. Blend in with your surroundings.

BABAR: A minute ago you were telling me to stand out from the crowd. Try rolling it the other way.

He takes the poster and rolls it the other way. It stays flat.

MR RIZVI: You know me, I'm very adaptable. I can change my views to reflect the situation in hand.

He holds out his hand and SALIM gives him some Blu-Tack. MR RIZVI sticks it onto the poster.

BABAR: You're fickle, you mean?

MR RIZVI: Flexible, not fickle. Yes, we have to act fast, let people know we're against these kinds of barbaric acts, before we become victims ourselves. I fear it might be too late even now. It hasn't even been two months since 9/11, but already Islamophobic attacks are on the increase. It's a terrifying time for everyone. I've warned your mother, too. There's been a lot of scarf snatching.

BABAR: At least people are interested in us.

MR RIZVI: That's not the kind of interest I want to attract. Negative interest. We should be seen as promoters of peace, not bloodthirsty butchers. Not that I'm denying there is a certain cruel streak to some of these maulvis. Imams are meant to inspire and teach us the beauty and the simplicity of Islam. Instead some of them do nothing but incite fear and hatred with their crazy talk of revenge and punishment.

BABAR: The imam from Wembley Mosque is your best friend.

MR RIZVI: I don't mean him. Dawood's an intelligent man.

BABAR: And I bet he's quite handy when it comes to getting together a nice, receptive audience.

MR RIZVI: Don't be cheeky. There are a lot of ambitious men who want to control the mosques – present company excluded, mind you – and so they import their often illiterate relatives from India and Pakistan and pass them off as maulana.

SALIM: Soon we'll have only puppets or fanatics to guide our souls. Or even fanatical puppets.

MR RIZVI: What we need in this country are British-born leaders. Someone who understands the society we live in. Home grown.

BABAR: What, like Mum's organic mint and tomatoes? You could start growing leaders along with the garden vegetables.

MR RIZVI: Your mother would like that.

SALIM: She'd probably take the job on herself.

MR RIZVI: The world's first female imam. I dread to think what she'd do with all that power…

He pulls a chair to the wall behind the sideboard and climbs on to it.

You know, if only people would listen to each other. It's so much more easy and pleasant than cursing and killing.

BABAR: Mental Muslims aren't the only murderers on the loose, Dad. There are plenty of legal massacres going on these days.

MR RIZVI: I agree with you, son. But it has to stop somewhere. And that's why our work is so important. Maybe in some small way we might be able to change something. My policies will be founded on all the wonderful aspects of our faith – charity, kindness, and being a good neighbour.

He gazes into the distance.

I see a thriving, loving community, a multicultural rainbow, where all the colours blend, harmonize, and complement each other. Write that down, quickly.

He turns and sticks the poster to the wall.

SALIM: You should ask Babar to write these speeches for you. I'm sure he's much more eloquent than I am.

MR RIZVI: Perhaps, but he doesn't understand me like you do. Now hurry, before we forget what it was I just said… That's it – blend, harmonize…and did I say fuse?

BABAR: Confuse.

MR RIZVI climbs down.

MR RIZVI: Be quiet if you can't help. (*To SALIM.*) Just put confuse. I mean fuse – for now, and we can go over it later. I have great visions for this place – I want to put Wembley on the map. It's going to be a shining example of a prospering, forward-thinking city, as well as a social hotspot. That's a good one too – make a note of it – social hotspot. I might forget it later.

BABAR: So what are your major concerns? Nightclubs and cinemas?

MR RIZVI: Of course not. There are many issues I care deeply about. I want to help set up a refuge for the victims of domestic violence – a terrible and very common problem. Our young people are a priority too – I'm going to support the new state-of-the-art youth centre. And being elected will help highlight my international fundraising activities.

BABAR: What saving up for your next holiday?

MR RIZVI: Be serious for once. We're trying to build a hospital in a small Pakistani village. It's desperately needed in the area.

BABAR: I remember hearing about that. I thought it was just something that you said to get people on side.

MR RIZVI: I try to do what I promise.

MR RIZVI looks at his picture.

It's not straight.

BABAR: It's alright.

MR RIZVI: No, no, no. It's better to have no poster at all than a wonky one. Lopsidedness is a symbol of imbalance. Disproportion. And there's none of that around here.

BABAR: Here, let me.

MR RIZVI: Oh, you don't know how I want it.

SALIM: I'll do it.

MR RIZVI: No, no –

SALIM: You can trust me. Look, I did the table alright, didn't I?

MR RIZVI looks at the table, and gives in. SALIM climbs on the chair and straightens the picture.

MR RIZVI: Did your mother like the suit?

SALIM: Yeah she was quite pleased. You should have bought her some jewellery to go with it.

MR RIZVI: I didn't think of it. Maybe you can get her something.

SALIM: No, you should choose it yourself. And you should go out somewhere together. You never do that. Have fun. Be a bit romantic.

MR RIZVI: Romantic? How can I be romantic with her? I was once. She was quite charming when she was young. That was before she slowly let religion overtake our lives. I'm a religious man myself, but you have to set your limits.

SALIM climbs down from the chair.

SALIM: How's that?

MR RIZVI: Wonderful. It's all coming together. The outside of the house is looking quite stunning too. The brass plaque was fitted onto the front door this morning. Have you seen it, Babar?

BABAR: What does it say?

MR RIZVI: Guess.

BABAR: Number 251?

MR RIZVI: No – it's a little more unique – but I won't spoil the surprise for you. Be sure to look at it later. And the new gravel for the drive – that was a last minute stroke of genius on my part. There's nothing more welcoming than that soothing, old fashioned crunch under the tyres as you drive up slowly towards a house. Did you move those plant pots from the porch?

SALIM: Mum doesn't like anyone touching those.

MR RIZVI: I'll have to move them myself then. Can't have the first impressions marred by something old and withered.

Exit MR RIZVI.

BABAR: Does he really think anyone wants him because of his policies?

SALIM: He's got a lot of valid points to make, you know.

BABAR: Please. Do you think the people voting bother to find out what they are? He's a brown face – that's all that matters to them – and his 'supporters' know it. He's as gullible as a baby. I don't like seeing my father being taken for a fool.

SALIM: He's happy enough.

BABAR: That's all you want, isn't it? For him to be happy. I suppose you haven't told him yet?

SALIM: Now's not a good time. He's got a lot of things on his mind.

BABAR: Who would have thought it, eh? Sensible Salim and his sordid little secret.

SALIM: It's not sordid! It's…pure.

BABAR: How is the little brat anyway?

SALIM: Haroon Thomas Jameel's very well, thanks.

BABAR: Where did the Thomas Jameel bit come from?

SALIM: It was Lisa's idea. She though it'd be respectful to add on our father's names. Well, Lisa wanted Thomas…

BABAR: So you stuck Jameel on the end to soften Grandad up. You better tell him yourself, Salim, before someone else does.

SALIM: She thinks I'm ashamed of her. But it's not that. I'm just trying to do what's best for everyone.

BABAR: You can't keep her hidden forever.

SALIM: I know. She's agreed to go through with the nikaah ceremony. We've arranged it for Friday with an imam in Hounslow. Once we're married it won't be so scandalous, and then I'll tell him. I just hope Lisa doesn't get any bright ideas before then.

Exit SALIM and BABAR.

SCENE 2

Enter MR RIZVI, in evening clothes, his bow-tie undone, around his neck. He is carrying a jacket on his arm. He puts it onto the back of the chair, and begins fiddling around with the food. He looks at the poster from different angles, then changes the position of a chair. Taking a notebook from his jacket, he walks to the front of the stage, and addresses an imaginary audience, reading from it.

MR RIZVI: I would like to start this evening by thanking you all for coming. I could not have even considered taking such a huge step into an unknown world had it not been for the love and support I have received from you all.

Enter AUNTY MOONA, carrying a handbag and several blue carrier bags with leafy bits of vegetable and coriander sticking out of the top. She has a plastic charity coin-box around her neck. She puts the shopping down and takes a sandwich, breaking it messily in half, eating one piece and putting the other back on the plate. He has not noticed her.

My story has a very humble beginning. Born in the backstreets of Karachi, I knew from childhood that I wanted to leave the droning, fruitless toil of that place behind me. And so, at the age of twenty-one, I left. I came to the city of…industry…and ball games…thirty years ago. I had nothing but the shirt on my back, and a suitcase full of dreams. (*Considering.*) Dreams? Hopes? Which sounds better?

AUNTY MOONA: Ambitions.

He spins round, startled.

MR RIZVI: What are you doing here?

She rattles the box at him.

AUNTY MOONA: Good deeds.

He sees she's been eating and snatches the sandwich from her.

Oh, Bhai saab!

MR RIZVI: You've ruined my arrangement.

He puts the paper on the table and starts to fix the plates of sandwiches.

AUNTY MOONA: I didn't know it was a special occasion today.

MR RIZVI: Well, it is. Some people of influence are coming for refreshments.

AUNTY MOONA: Really? That's good. But you should have told me earlier. I don't have much time to get ready.

MR RIZVI: What for?

AUNTY MOONA: To meet the people of influence.

MR RIZVI: You don't understand. It's a private function.

AUNTY MOONA: Private is good. It stops any old rabble from coming in. But your tie, Bhai saab – do you need help? I can do it for you.

She starts doing up his tie.

I've always wanted to do one of these. They look so elegant.

MR RIZVI: (*Gasping slightly.*) Too tight, too tight!

AUNTY MOONA: Don't fuss! A little pain for a little pleasure. There.

She pats his chest. She has made a mess. MRS RIZVI has entered.

MRS RIZVI: Moona!

AUNTY MOONA jumps.

After everything I've told you about him – you should be ashamed of yourself.

AUNTY MOONA: It's alright, Safia. Bhai saab just asked me to give him the hand.

MR RIZVI: No, no –

MRS RIZVI: I believe you. He's always the one to make the first move. (*To MR RIZVI.*) Think you look smart, eh, wearing the dress of the devil? Hitch up your trousers!

MR RIZVI: I'm not in the mosque now.

MRS RIZVI: But it's still nice to be righteously clothed. Your ankles are not visible beneath those pyjamas of disbelief.

MR RIZVI: Put on a pair of shorts, shall I?

MRS RIZVI: Yes, as long as they cover your knees.

MR RIZVI: Well, Moona –

MRS RIZVI: Sister Moona, if you please.

MR RIZVI: Of course. Sister Moona. Thank you very much for your help. As you can see we are busy, so we would really like to get on.

AUNTY MOONA: I'll just go home and get changed also.

MR RIZVI: Moona, we have a very select guest list tonight and I don't think your name is on it.

AUNTY MOONA: Oh. That's a shame. You know I'm collecting for the new Urdu school they are setting up. (*Shakes the box.*) Your guests might have been impressed to hear about your input to the local community.

MR RIZVI: Well…alright, maybe one person won't make a difference. Maybe I should make a donation first.

He puts some money into her box.

And you do know that I'm involved with several other organisations too?

AUNTY MOONA: I know, I'll tell everyone.

MR RIZVI: The Pakistani hospital, and the Heart Foundation.

AUNTY MOONA: Dating agency?

MR RIZVI: No, no, health research.

AUNTY MOONA: Acha, acha, medical science. Very good.

MRS RIZVI: Why don't you ask Bashir Bhai to come with you?

MR RIZVI is annoyed.

AUNTY MOONA: He's asleep.

MR RIZVI: Already? Well, never mind, don't disturb him.

AUNTY MOONA: He's on the night shift at the moment. He sleeps as I live through my day. My jobs must be done in the morning – shopping, cleaning, cooking.

MR RIZVI: Well maybe next time. And remember, don't bring the box with you. It's a bit…distracting. It might confuse people – they're not expecting to be giving money away.

AUNTY MOONA: I understand. I'm always very gentle. I know that you can't force people into generosity.

She takes out her purse and takes out some coins, which she gives to MRS RIZVI.

AUNTY MOONA: Here's your change. The kadoo were mouldy and the lamb chops were finished. Everything else is in there.

MRS RIZVI: Thank you.

AUNTY MOONA: Maybe tomorrow we can go to Southall and get a few things.

MRS RIZVI: No. I don't think so.

AUNTY MOONA: You will enjoy it. I will be there to look after you.

MRS RIZVI: No, Moona, leave it.

AUNTY MOONA: Okay. I will see you later then.

Exit AUNTY MOONA.

MR RIZVI: She's always so…interested in everything. (*Beat.*) Did you like the outfit?

MRS RIZVI: I'm wearing it, aren't I?

MR RIZVI: I'm glad. The colour suits you. I wanted you to look nice for tonight.

MRS RIZVI: Worried I might show you up by appearing in my old rags, were you?

MR RIZVI: No, that's not what I meant, Safia.

Beat.

Salim was suggesting we go out – maybe for dinner.

MRS RIZVI: I don't want to force you into anything. Anyway, it's too late now.

MR RIZVI: I didn't mean tonight.

MRS RIZVI: Neither did I.

Beat.

So, how many of them are coming tonight?

MR RIZVI: Who?

MRS RIZVI: You know who I mean. Those charels. [*Witches.*] Witches.

MR RIZVI: If you mean the lady members of my political circle, then there will be five such respectable persons present. I expect you to treat them with the courtesy all our guests deserve.

MRS RIZVI: They're not my guests.

MR RIZVI: Safia, please.

MRS RIZVI: I'll get to the bottom of it soon. I'll find out exactly what's been going on.

MR RIZVI: Nothing, apart from a little friendship.

MRS RIZVI: So you admit it?

MR RIZVI: Admit what? Look, just be nice to everyone. That's all I'm asking. And they're lovely ladies once you get to know them.

MRS RIZVI: Which you obviously have.

MR RIZVI: What's happened to you? Please stop this. Everyone will be here soon.

MRS RIZVI: Here to spread their poison.

MR RIZVI: Don't say these things.

MRS RIZVI: My morals compel me to do so.

MR RIZVI: Morals? What morals? Morals aren't founded on lies and suspicion, Safia.

He goes out, leaving her. She notices he has left his jacket on the chair. She looks through the pockets and takes out a notebook. She looks through it, stops on a page, reads it, then snaps it shut. She picks up the bags and goes, taking the diary with her.

SCENE 3

It is the party. MR RIZVI is standing by the sideboard, taking care not to obscure his poster from view. He's wearing a red rose in his buttonhole. AUNTY MOONA is standing with a plate in her hand and her coin-box around her neck. There is something to suggest the impression of a lot of people, maybe a soundtrack in the background of people talking. SALIM is standing and addressing the audience as though they are the guests.

SALIM: Well, thanks to all of you for coming. It's been a real pleasure to see so many of you here tonight, and I hope it's just the beginning of what will become a regular tradition in the future. Now, I know that my father wants to say a few words, so I'll hand over to him without further ado. Dad?

MR RIZVI steps forward.

MR RIZVI: Oh, thank you, thank you. I would like to start this evening by thanking you all for coming…

He is fumbling in his pockets for his notebook.

I'm sorry. Strange. My speech has disappeared – not literally of course, you can see I'm still fully functioning in that sense. (*Laughs at his own joke.*) Well…honest words come from within, not from notebooks. I came to this city of industry and ball games thirty years ago with nothing but a suitcase full of dreams. Now I have a modestly successful business, a great family, and wonderful friends. I feel it's time for me to give something back to the community that has blessed me with so much. One of my main concerns is the problem of domestic violence, and if I am elected I will be doing my best to tackle it. I will also be doing my best to secure more funding for our schools – something many of you have expressed a lot of interest in.

AUNTY MOONA begins to clap loudly as MRS RIZVI enters. She is dressed entirely in black, in a long, cloak-type garment, with a scarf on her head.

AUNTY MOONA: Ah, here is Safia, his dearest wife. Go, Safia, jao, stand beside him.

AUNTY MOONA pulls her and stands her next to MR RIZVI. She claps some more.

Say thanks to wife and family. Safia, you say something, too.

The doorbell rings.

I'll get it.

Exit AUNTY MOONA.

MR RIZVI: I'm sure you've all met my…lovely wife. Er, it's true that behind every successful man is the hand of a good woman.

MRS RIZVI: Or, as in this case, the hands of several bad women. Behind, under, in, all over.

MR RIZVI: Er, yes, Safia's got a real sense of humour, as you can see. Well, I have plenty more to say but now's the time to enjoy yourselves. Please all go through to the drawing room and help yourself to some refreshments. (*To BABAR.*) Go and put some music on. Something relaxing. What do you think they'll like?

BABAR: You always listen to Ghulam Ali.

MR RIZVI: Don't be silly. I think there's a Mozart CD in there somewhere.

Exit BABAR. MR RIZVI shuts the door behind him. To MRS RIZVI.

Why did you say that? And why are you wearing this? What happened to the suit I gave you? I thought you liked it.

MRS RIZVI: You know I like to preserve my modesty in public.

MR RIZVI: That's all very well but there's no need to give people the creeps! This – it's a reminder of…other places that we don't want to think about. The whole point of all this was to try and make them forget… Just for once you could have made an effort, for my sake.

MRS RIZVI: I did, once. But you didn't see. All those evenings waiting, making myself beautiful for eyes that were closed.

MR RIZVI: What? Don't start with the riddles, now, please. Just try and have some fun.

He takes a drink.

MRS RIZVI: Leave that for the unbelievers. There's a nice selection of fizzy drinks over there – cherryade and cream soda.

She takes the drink away and exits to the kitchen. Mozart begins to play in the background. MR RIZVI helps himself to another drink. Enter SALIM.

SALIM: They're waiting, Dad.

AUNTY MOONA enters.

AUNTY MOONA: There's a woman at the door, called Aleesa, Aneesa, something, demanding to be let in. I did what I could – I wrestled with her, I pinned her to the wall, I told her this was a private party, VIPs only but –

SALIM: I'll go, you stay here.

AUNTY MOONA: But let me warn you –

SALIM: Don't worry about it.

Exit SALIM.

AUNTY MOONA: He didn't let me warn him. I better tell you instead. She was very angry – she was upset she wasn't invited.

MR RIZVI: Really? Who could it be? I'm sure I invited everybody important. Unless…it's a member of the opposition. Oh, they'll resort to anything. Well, it's original at least. A political spy disguised as a gatecrasher. I'll see to it.

AUNTY MOONA: I don't think you should.

MR RIZVI: I know what I'm doing.

He tries to go but she stops him.

AUNTY MOONA: Let Salim do the dealing.

MR RIZVI: He's a bit inexperienced – he might be taken in.

AUNTY MOONA: Trust me, Bhai saab. I think Salim knows best in this case. For your own sake, stick with me. Come here.

They are close together as if sharing a secret.

I think this is a different problem.

MR RIZVI: How do you know?

AUNTY MOONA: She was upset.

MR RIZVI: Yes.

AUNTY MOONA: She was angry.

MR RIZVI: Yes.

AUNTY MOONA: Because she wasn't invited.

MR RIZVI: Yes, yes, you told me. Next bit.

AUNTY MOONA: She said she had a claim on the family.

MR RIZVI: What do you mean, a claim on the family? Was she threatening blackmail?

AUNTY MOONA: Chup, Bhai saab not so loud.

MR RIZVI: Tell me then.

AUNTY MOONA: Perhaps I shouldn't have mentioned.

MR RIZVI: Well you have mentioned, so come on.

AUNTY MOONA: Somebody was asking for samosas.

MR RIZVI: Who?

AUNTY MOONA: An honourable lady in a pink dress.

MR RIZVI: Was she? I didn't expect that. Maybe I can order some from the takeaway.

AUNTY MOONA: Oh don't worry, I gave her my home address, and told her she is welcome any time. My own cooking is better than takeaway...

MR RIZVI goes to the sideboard and opens the drawers.

MR RIZVI: Where is the *Yellow Pages*? Help me look for it.

AUNTY MOONA: Frozen ones are also good value. Of course, you have to fry them yourself.

MR RIZVI: Find it, hurry.

AUNTY MOONA gets on her knees and looks under the table. MR RIZVI is also crawling on the floor looking under the sideboard. BABAR enters.

44

BABAR: What are you doing?

MR RIZVI: Do you know where the *Yellow Pages* is?

BABAR gets it out from under the coffee table. MR RIZVI looks through it quickly, still on the floor.

MR RIZVI: Karahi restaurant, tandoori, tandoori, haa, yeh chale gaa. [*This will do.*] Red Rose Indian Takeaway. Moona, go and check if they need anything else, and report back to me with any more special requests.

Exit AUNTY MOONA. MR RIZVI dials and speaks into the phone.

Haa, yes, er, do you deliver samosas? Good, that's very good. I would like a hundred samosas, please, as soon as possible. You can do it? The address? 251 Allendale Drive. Wembley. It says Villa Rizvi above the door. Yes, Villa. Oh yaar, V, I, L, L, A. No, no, V for vegetable not B for banana. Forget it, just write 251. Soon as possible please.

Puts the phone down. To BABAR.

Someone asked for samosas.

BABAR: You don't have to give them everything they want.

MR RIZVI: Yes, yes, it's good PR.

He gets up and fixes his appearance hurriedly.

Look at your clothes.

BABAR: What? I put a suit on, what else do you want?

MR RIZVI: I don't like the pattern of this jacket. Too gaudy. Haven't you seen Salim's? Get something like that next time. A much neater design. Now, what have you been doing all evening? Did you meet everyone? What about

Mr Willoughby? A very nice gentleman indeed. Go and introduce yourself to him. I'll be there in a minute.

Exit BABAR. MR RIZVI starts looking for his notebook. Enter AUNTY MOONA.

AUNTY MOONA: Only request is for your humble presence.

MR RIZVI: Have you seen my notebook?

AUNTY MOONA: Notebook is not necessary now. You just grace us with your presence.

MR RIZVI: Yes but that book – it's got some personal jottings in it. I wouldn't want anybody picking it up. You know how these journalists make sleaze out of the most innocent things. Maybe that's who was at the door…

AUNTY MOONA: Oh, she's no journalist, Bhai saab! I'll let you know if I find your diary. But just hurry up now, or you'll miss the moment of glory!

She starts dragging him from the room. Enter SALIM. MR RIZVI breaks free of AUNTY MOONA.

MR RIZVI: Wait. Who was it, Salim? Who was she? You didn't tell her anything, did you? Well? Come on, spit it out! I haven't got all night!

AUNTY MOONA: Maybe he's shy.

MR RIZVI: What?

AUNTY MOONA: Boys are shy about these things with their fathers.

MR RIZVI: Look, Moona, Salim, I'm really beginning to lose my patience. Speak, someone!

AUNTY MOONA: People have been saying, Bhai saab…

MR RIZVI: What have they been saying?

AUNTY MOONA: About beta Salim and his lady friend.

MR RIZVI: Really Moona! I'm surprised you listen to these things. And don't go and repeat this silly rumour inside. You're not offended are you Salim?

SALIM: It's true, Dad. The girl at the door – it was Lisa. Me and Lisa… We're getting married. (*Beat.*) Dad, I know this isn't a good time to tell you the news but –

MR RIZVI: You're damn right it's not.

SALIM: I'm sorry. I mean sorry for springing it on you like this.

Pause.

I wanted to tell you before, honestly, Dad, but it was just finding the right time. We're having our nikaah ceremony next week. So it'll be official. What do you think, Dad?

MR RIZVI: Tumhara dimagh kharaab ho gaya hai? [*Have you lost your mind?*]

Enter BABAR.

BABAR: Dad, people are wondering where you've got to.

MR RIZVI: I can't face them now.

BABAR: Why not?

MR RIZVI: I was just talking to Mr Anjum from Bradford. I invited him to bring his daughter round for dinner. To meet you, Salim. Now I won't be able to look him in the eye!

SALIM: Dad!

MR RIZVI: Unless…if you keep quiet, he might never find out. He lives in Yorkshire, maybe he hasn't got many contacts on the Wembley grapevine. And he's very keen.

It must be the prestige of being attached to a public persona…

SALIM: Dad, please listen to me…

MR RIZVI: It's not a bad deal for us either. She's a very intelligent girl. She's studied law. I'll go and talk to Anjum now.

SALIM: We've got a son.

MR RIZVI: What? What did he say?

SALIM: We've got a son.

Silence.

Dad?

MR RIZVI leaps onto him and starts attacking him.

MR RIZVI: Haramzaada! Cutta! [*Bastard! Dog!*]

AUNTY MOONA grabs him, pushes him onto the chair, and maybe muffles his mouth so he can't speak, as BABAR pulls SALIM away.

AUNTY MOONA: Keep the knickers on straight, Bhai saab.

MR RIZVI: Trying to be Daddy's pet and all the time deceiving me!

AUNTY MOONA: Quiet! They will hear. Now sit down. Bhai saab, he is your son. Don't be too angry with him.

MR RIZVI: That's not the way sons behave. I trusted him. He's been cheating on me.

BABAR: He was only thinking of you, Dad.

MR RIZVI: What?

BABAR: There's always something stressing you out. He just didn't want to make it worse.

AUNTY MOONA: You're lucky, Bhai saab, he is so considerate about your feelings. Otherwise today's children don't about their parents. They wear you out and then cast you away like an old pair of shoes. I know.

MR RIZVI: Can't you see this…woman is just after your money?

SALIM: Don't talk about her like that.

BABAR: Calm down, both of you. Can you get him some water, please, Aunty?

AUNTY MOONA: I won't let you dehydrate.

Exit AUNTY MOONA.

MR RIZVI: What will I do? I'm ruined.

BABAR: It's not that bad, Dad. You could put a positive twist onto it. Set an example. Promote the 'global family'.

MR RIZVI: Global family! Huh! (*Then thinks.*) Actually, I quite like the sound of that. After all, I am known for encouraging multi-lingual mingling. Hmm… But no! Next week I'm going on a tour of all the mosques in the borough. What a hypocrite I'll look.

AUNTY MOONA comes back and hands him the water. He drinks it and hands it back to her.

Thank you.

MRS RIZVI enters.

MRS RIZVI: Party still in full swing?

MR RIZVI: Oh yes. Salim has some good news for you dear. Come and sit down. Babar, go and make sure everything is alright. Keep an eye out for eavesdroppers.

Exti BABAR. She sits down.

SALIM: We can talk about this later.

MR RIZVI: Tell her now, Salim.

MRS RIZVI: Is something wrong?

AUNTY MOONA: Very exciting news, Safia.

MRS RIZVI: Have you won the lottery? You know I don't approve of gambling.

SALIM: I'm getting married, Mum.

MRS RIZVI: That's very good. About time. Moona knows lots of nice girls.

MR RIZVI: No need to waste time on that. He's already chosen his bride.

MRS RIZVI: Salim! You didn't tell me! When will you bring her to see me?

MR RIZVI: Her name is Lisa.

MRS RIZVI: Our people have become so modern. What sort of name is that for a Muslim girl? Probably short for something. These days even Mohammeds call themselves Mike.

MR RIZVI: What's her surname, Salim?

SALIM: Lisa Owens. She's English, Mum.

MRS RIZVI: Salim! How could you do this to me? After all I've taught you… I tried to help you towards the right way…

SALIM: We love each other.

MRS RIZVI: Oh, love! It's a hard thing to catch and even harder to keep.

Pause.

Is she Christian?

SALIM: Well…yeah.

MRS RIZVI: Legally you are allowed a Christian wife. You've stayed inside the rules. Just.

MR RIZVI: Safia!

MRS RIZVI: If she converts, then he will be rewarded.

MR RIZVI: Let's see what he'll get for his other little surprise then. Salim?

Pause.

You've got a little grandson, too, dear.

MRS RIZVI: What a spiteful thing to say about your own child! Salim, why are you tolerating such talk? Salim? It's not…true? Tell me it's not! It is… You have…

SALIM: Mum…

He tries to put his hand on her arm but she moves away.

MRS RIZVI: Don't touch me! You're not clean. Get off!

She moves even further away from him and sits down away from them all. She takes out her beads, and starts to whisper over them. Pause. AUNTY MOONA goes to comfort her but MRS RIZVI ignores her.

MR RIZVI: Salim, where is the girl now?

SALIM: She's gone home.

MR RIZVI: You have to promise not to see her again until after the election.

SALIM: You know I won't do that.

MR RIZVI: At least promise not to say anything then. I don't think there's any way of making it look like a plus point.

AUNTY MOONA: I know something about public relations from my charity work. If you need a spin-doctor I can give you some ideas. How about this? 'Straight laced Muslim candidate shows his cheeky rebel streak…'? Or: 'He's just a normal guy like you. The house, the wife, the illegitimate grandchild…'

Pause.

MR RIZVI: I don't think you should be involved in the campaign any more Salim. Just to be on the safe side. You'll have to go.

SALIM: You can't do that, Dad. After all the work I've put into this.

MR RIZVI: The work is useless if it doesn't get us what we want. Later, when things are calmer, you can come back.

MRS RIZVI: It will be acceptable once he's won his election. But not in front of God… I can pray for you, but that's all.

MR RIZVI: Meanwhile, I'll need a new PA.

AUNTY MOONA: My charity job is only part time. If you're prepared to be flexible then I'd be happy to take on the job.

Enter BABAR.

BABAR: Dad, are you coming or not?

MR RIZVI: Yes, yes. It's too late to make any enquiries at this time, Salim. Get onto it first thing in the morning. I'm sure if you ring around someone will come up.

BABAR: What for? What's happening?

AUNTY MOONA: Your brother is getting in the sack.

MR RIZVI: I'm not sacking him. Think of it as an early holiday, Salim.

AUNTY MOONA: It will give you time to get ready for the big day.

MR RIZVI: What am I thinking of? The perfect solution is here before my eyes.

AUNTY MOONA is pleased. She thinks he means her.

MR RIZVI: (*To BABAR.*) You will take over from Salim.

BABAR: Me?

SALIM: He doesn't know anything about this sort of thing.

MR RIZVI: You can teach him. What do you say, Babar?

BABAR: It's not really the way I work. And I don't think you should tell Salim to leave just because of this.

MR RIZVI: I know you'd like to contribute your own ideas. Any of your suggestions will be welcomed and carefully considered.

BABAR: I was going to take a more practical approach.

MR RIZVI: I'm having leaflets and flyers printed. You're welcome to distribute them if you want. Maybe you could help with that, Salim.

SALIM: Oh, thanks.

BABAR: You don't understand, Dad. I won't be here. I'm going away for a while.

MR RIZVI: You can go sightseeing at any time, son. But I need you now. And this is a good opportunity for you.

BABAR: I'm not going on holiday. I'm going to join the fight.

MR RIZVI: What fight?

The doorbell rings. AUNTY MOONA goes out.

BABAR: The one organised by your new friends in Westminster. The one that's turning our brothers and sisters into orphans and widows and corpses.

MR RIZVI: I find your joke in poor taste, Babar. War and death are not laughing matters. Now, back to the topic in hand. When can you start?

BABAR: I'm serious, Dad.

AUNTY MOONA returns.

AUNTY MOONA: It's the samosa man. He won't hand them over until you pay up.

MR RIZVI takes out some money and gives it to her.

MR RIZVI: Now tell me, what are you talking about? Where did you get this idea from?

Silence.

Salim? Did you know about this? Who has he been talking to?

SALIM: He's been hanging around with the new imam in Alperton. Sheikh Mahmood.

MR RIZVI: What? Why didn't you stop him, Salim?

SALIM: I didn't know until last week.

MR RIZVI: You should have kept an eye on him.

SALIM: I'm not his minder.

MR RIZVI: That man is a fanatic.

BABAR: He's just passionate. Maybe he goes a bit far sometimes, but he's got the right idea.

MR RIZVI: These snakes with their slippery tongues are making maniacs out of our youth. They take the naïve and fill them with guilt and madness. But you, at least, have some intelligence. A brain that works.

BABAR: I don't see any madness in stopping the slaughter of innocent people.

MR RIZVI: You can't be serious. How much slaughter are you going to stop? You'll do more harm than good. Over there and over here. It's hard enough for us as it is. Do you know what it took just to get them here tonight?

BABAR: Is that all you care about? A good image? When hundreds of people are dying?

MR RIZVI: No, of course not. But what you're saying won't achieve anything.

BABAR: It's our duty to help our brothers. Isn't it, Mum?

MRS RIZVI: We must help them, yes, but…

MR RIZVI: I suppose it's your duty to blow up civilians too is it? To send all non-believers to hell?

BABAR: I didn't say that.

MR RIZVI: But I bet your friend the Sheikh did. What does he really teach you about Islam? God says that killing even one man is like killing the whole of humanity. I don't suppose he told you that did he, when he was training you to go on this suicide mission?

BABAR: As you said, I do have a brain that works. I don't believe everything he says. I'm not going on a suicide mission with a bomb in my backpack. Those people are utterly defenceless. They've got nowhere to go. They wait for death to drop out of the sky. Have you forgotten that God also says protect yourselves from those who attack you and your homes?

MR RIZVI: This is your home, Babar! Here!

SALIM: What does home mean?

MR RIZVI: Salim! You're supposed to be helping me. Go inside for a while and make sure they're alright. Talk to the chairman of the Ladies' Rugby Club about future partnership possibilities. And don't breathe a word of this.

Exit SALIM. AUNTY MOONA enters with a platter piled high with samosas.

AUNTY MOONA: He didn't bring any chutney. So stingy.

She holds one up.

Anyone to try before I take them in?

Nobody answers so she eats it herself.

BABAR: Would you sit here smiling over tea and cakes and cocktails if they invaded Pakistan?

MR RIZVI: That's different.

BABAR: How?

MR RIZVI: Look, you're not going anywhere. It's ridiculous. Tell him, Safia.

MRS RIZVI hesitates.

MRS RIZVI: You should listen to him, beta. He's right, for once. You can't just rush off like this on an impulse.

BABAR: I've thought it through, Mum. I thought you'd be pleased I'm doing what I believe in.

MRS RIZVI: I am, but it's too dangerous.

BABAR: I can't let fear change my convictions. You never have.

MRS RIZVI: That's a different thing. My religion is about…controlling yourself…obeying God, reading namaaz, not risking my life.

BABAR: You mean it's all just theory? Isn't our religion – any religion – fundamentally about humanity? We're making empty prayers if we live without compassion, or mercy, or love. Isn't it a dead kind of worship if we aren't alive to each other?

MRS RIZVI: What are you saying, Babar? I don't understand… Just don't leave me. Already I have so little.

BABAR: I'm not the only one. There are three others. They've been blessed by their mothers.

MRS RIZVI: The mothers?

BABAR: Yes.

MRS RIZVI: Blessed them? Sent their children, willingly, to…to fight…or worse?

Pause.

They will be rewarded, yes, both mothers and sons… But I don't know if I can…

Moment of silence.

MR RIZVI: Of course you can't. He's your son. (*He is nodding with approval.*) You're not like those others, forgetting everything to indulge in this idiocy, this obsessive lunacy they call religion! See, Babar? Even your mother agrees with me.

MRS RIZVI: (*Almost in a whisper.*) What did you say? What did you call it?

MR RIZVI: I think you are making a very wise decision, dear –

MRS RIZVI: Will you be careful? Do you promise to come back?

BABAR: I can't promise that, Mum.

MR RIZVI: What are you saying, Safia?

MRS RIZVI: If anything happens…they call them martyrs.

MR RIZVI: Fools! They call them fools.

MRS RIZVI: Martyrs.

MR RIZVI: Safia! Tum paagal to nahi ho gaye? [*Have you gone completely mad?*]

MRS RIZVI: A noble death is better than a shameful life. You have my blessing, son.

She kisses BABAR's hand, and then turns to the dining table. She starts picking up glasses and putting them on the tray.

Empty. All of them. Drained.

She holds a glass up.

Sapped dry.

She turns it upside down and a drop falls out. She goes out with the tray.

AUNTY MOONA: Beta, I don't think you understand the situation. The Americans are only helping. They want to get rid of evil dictators and bad governments. The Afghan people love them. I saw them on the news, saying thank you for saving our land. I say George Bush zindabaad.

MR RIZVI: Doesn't this country mean anything to you? It's given you everything. Now we are even accepted as a valuable part of the society.

BABAR: And how much does acceptance cost, Dad? Did you pay for it with your conscience? It's not just about it being our countries, our people. I won't say that doesn't matter. But in the end, it's about doing what's right.

MR RIZVI: I know how you feel, son, believe me. But jihad doesn't have to be with the sword – any struggle in the way of God is a jihad. In today's world we must use other ways of spreading our message. Believe me, we're really beginning to make some progress.

BABAR: But we don't save lives, do we?

MR RIZVI: We will save lives – together. We will protest, we will write letters, we will make them listen. I've spent my life trying to build bridges of understanding between cultures. Everything will collapse in your one moment of insanity.

BABAR: What's your cause compared to all that death and destruction? It's called sacrifice, Dad, something you know nothing about.

MR RIZVI: Don't you understand that it's not only my cause? And don't talk to me about sacrifices. You think I haven't given anything up, my freedom, staying here, married to the high priestess? Forever being subjected to her fatal fatwas? You'll roast on God's barbecue if you eat a bacon crisp. You'll be thrown into hot oil for smiling at a strange woman. What do you think it's been like for me, being forced into a life of piety? Safia's never understood that true faith has to come from the heart.

BABAR: So why have you stayed all this time?

MR RIZVI: It's not only mothers that will do anything for their children.

Pause.

Babar, the killing, the craziness has to stop somewhere… Stay and we will fight together.

BABAR is coming round to the idea.

AUNTY MOONA: When is your ticket flying?

BABAR: I was going on Friday…

AUNTY MOONA: Hai!

She crosses her hands over her chest melodramatically.

Shall I help you with packing?

MR RIZVI: Why don't you take those in?

Exit AUNTY MOONA.

You've seen who's here tonight. It's been quite productive, all things considered. You'll be a part of our 'family' too. Salim can be your mentor.

Pause.

BABAR: I can't do what you do. I can't beg.

MR RIZVI turns away. Offstage, trays clatter to the floor.

SCENE 4

BABAR is on the sofa with a bag and some papers, his passport and general travel items. He's putting things into the bag. SALIM enters. He's carrying files which he puts on the table and begins to sort through.

BABAR: You've got a lot of work to do for someone who's on 'unofficial holiday'.

SALIM: Someone's got to do it.

BABAR: What does Lisa think about all this?

SALIM: She doesn't understand. She'd prefer it if I just left. But Dad needs me too. And it's not nice having your reputation destroyed.

BABAR: It's not nice living like a dirty secret.

SALIM: Maybe if there was someone else around… I could spend more time with her if there wasn't so much to do.

BABAR: Get a secretary.

SALIM: You don't have to do it, Babar.

BABAR: I've got no intention of learning shorthand.

SALIM: You know what I'm talking about. There are other ways.

BABAR: What other ways, Salim? We've tried going on marches and writing letters and signing petitions. We see murder every day and all we do is shake our heads and change the channel.

SALIM: But what good are you going to be? You haven't got a clue what it's like out there.

BABAR: You're right. I haven't. That's why I have to go, to see for myself. To see the truth. Maybe when I get there, I won't do anything. I don't know. But if I stay here, I'll go mad. I feel like my mind's being crushed when I think about it. Sitting here playing on the computer, writing out postcards…it's not enough.

SALIM: Just wait and see what happens. If Dad gets this – you can work with him and do what you like. It's what he wants.

BABAR: No he doesn't. He doesn't want me – he wants another you.

SALIM: He just likes me because he thinks I agree with him all the time. But you'd be surprised how many of his big ideas started out as my little suggestions. You can show him new things – and I'll make sure he listens.

BABAR: Yeah, but he never hears me.

SALIM: He loves you. He can't stand you going like this.

BABAR: Why, what's he said?

SALIM: He hasn't been concentrating on his work properly. He looks lost. He forgets things.

BABAR: Probably just worried about his results. Well, what did he say?

SALIM: Nothing, but I know what's going on in his head.

BABAR shakes his head. Pause.

He even went to see Lisa yesterday. And Haroon. He loved him. He had a great big smile on his face – I haven't seen that in a while.

BABAR: Haven't you?

He looks at the poster.

SALIM: Then Lisa suggested he take Haroon for a walk down the high street. It's not funny. At least he tried. But Mum – that's another story.

BABAR: Why don't you try the magic of Haroon Thomas on her?

SALIM: Yeah, I did. I showed her some photos. She doesn't mind him. It's me she's got the problem with. She treats me like I'm diseased. God knows what's going to happen when you go. You're killing her...

BABAR: But it's one of her and thousands of them.

SALIM: What's it going to take to make you stay?

Pause. Maybe they hug.

AUNTY MOONA: (*Offstage.*) Yoo hoo! Where is everyone?

SALIM: If you can face the next five minutes alone, you can face anything.

He goes. AUNTY MOONA enters.

AUNTY MOONA: I've just bought some *bon voyage* goodies for the traveller. Have you got a bum bag?

She takes out a fluorescent pouch and holds it up to show him. She begins tying it round his waist.

It will be very useful during the flight. And it's glow-in-the-dark. It might even come in handy later, when you... It will help with night vision. Yes, that looks very smart. Now what else? Here are some travel sickness sweets...and here is ten pounds for you to spend.

BABAR: No, Aunty, I can't take that.

AUNTY MOONA: Take it, beta, take it.

Presses him with the money.

BABAR: No, Aunty, please.

AUNTY MOONA: Come on, don't upset your aunty.

BABAR: You keep it. Put it in your charity box.

AUNTY MOONA: Okay.

She puts the money away.

If you insist. I'll give you one of these instead then.

She pulls out a roll of stickers from her coat and slaps it onto him.

All ready to go?

BABAR: Yeah, just about.

Pause.

AUNTY MOONA: I know you think I am a nosy woman. But I have to tell you this. I have given you gifts, but if you ask me the truth – you are making a mistake.

BABAR: I know you're a big fan of George W –

AUNTY MOONA: Forget about Dubya. I am a fan but that's not the point. I'm talking about Safia.

BABAR: Mum's alright. She's agreed to it.

AUNTY MOONA: No, no, beta. No woman can be happy about something like this. It's hard enough for a mother when she sends her child to school for the first time. What do you think this will do to her?

BABAR: Mum's strong. And she's got you to look after her.

AUNTY MOONA: Yes I look after her well. But I cannot replace you. You are young. You don't know what mothers feel. Ask me. I know about the pain. I haven't seen my son for six months and he only lives in Greenford. His wife has taken him away from me…

She is getting tearful.

Last week I saw him in the meat shop. He hid behind a pile of Asli Atta to avoid me…

BABAR comforts her.

Please, beta. Safia is like my own sister. I don't want to see her suffer. And you – I have watched you grow up. You are like my son. Please don't do this to us.

BABAR: It'll be alright, Aunty. Who's the shiny present for?

AUNTY MOONA: Oh dear. I forgot the most important thing. You will like it. Open.

He opens it. It is a large doll dressed as a soldier, holding a Union Jack.

I know, I know, you don't like the flag. I didn't have time to make a new one. Get me some scissors. I'll cut it off for you.

BABAR: No, that's fine. I don't have a problem with the flag. It's very nice, thank you.

AUNTY MOONA: You haven't even seen what it does yet. Watch.

She puts the doll on the floor and presses it. It begins marching and singing the song, 'We Will Rock You'. She starts clapping to the music.

Lovely isn't it?

Looks at him in a sneaky way.

BABAR: Yeah, it's great. Thanks.

AUNTY MOONA: How does it make you feel? Cheerful…? Happy…? Maybe, proud?

BABAR: Patriotic?

AUNTY MOONA: Maybe, yes, could be.

BABAR: Nice try, Aunty.

AUNTY MOONA: You are a very stubborn boy. If you must have your way, then promise to be careful.

BABAR: I promise. I don't know if this will fit in the suitcase.

AUNTY MOONA: I'll take it home for safekeeping then. Let me just have another go.

She turns on the doll again. MRS RIZVI enters. She is carrying a towel.

MRS RIZVI: What's that noise? Turn it off!

AUNTY MOONA turns it off.

AUNTY MOONA: Babar beta, I am going now. Your uncle will be waking up and wanting his dinner before he goes to work.

She gets up.

We will be praying. And your little soldier will be here waiting for you when you come back.

She pats his head affectionately. She leaves, taking the doll with her. MRS RIZVI gives BABAR the towel.

MRS RIZVI: Take this with you. I've washed it. Have you taken enough clothes? You'll need sweaters. Lots of sweaters. I have your father's thermals if you want those.

BABAR: And what will Dad do?

MRS RIZVI: He can freeze.

BABAR smiles at her.

BABAR: He probably needs the long johns more than I do. I'll survive.

She unpacks the bag.

MRS RIZVI: What a mess you've made.

She is taking everything out.

BABAR: You don't need to take everything out just for one towel.

MRS RIZVI: I need to check you have got everything you need. And make sure there are no breakables at the bottom. Some things are very delicate. They smash easily. And then they are beyond repair.

Pause.

BABAR: Mum, try and get on with Dad. He's not that bad. He does care about you.

MRS RIZVI: You boys will say anything to keep me quiet.

BABAR: I'm saying it because it's true.

MRS RIZVI: He's got a funny way of showing it.

Pause.

You know, when we first got married he used to buy me roses every Friday. There used to be a boy selling them outside his office. Red rosebuds. I would put them in water and watch them open up into gorgeous big blooms… And then the foolish first love faded and he got busier and busier… In the end he got lost trying to 'light the way forward'. Now he doesn't even remember my birthday.

Pause. By now she has put everything back in. She starts taking it all out again.

BABAR: You need to talk to each other.

MRS RIZVI: I've told him many times that he is wrong –

BABAR: Talk, and listen, not argue.

MRS RIZVI: He knows where I am. And anyway, why are you telling me? How many times have you spoken to him in the last two days?

BABAR: I tried yesterday. I tried to explain. He didn't say anything. He put on a pair of headphones and started listening to Whitney Houston.

MRS RIZVI: Then you know what he's like.

BABAR: Well this is a bit different. I can understand why he's upset with me. Mum what are you doing?

She's jumbled all the clothes up.

MRS RIZVI: Oh dear. I think you might have to cancel your flight. Your bag is not packed. You'll be late. You'll miss the plane.

Beat.

I know I should be happy. That's the right way to feel for a woman in my position.

BABAR: Try not to worry about it, Mum. I'll be okay.

MRS RIZVI: Tell me – truthfully – do you think you are right? Leaving me like this? So alone. You will make me a grieving mother. And if you kill – so many more will become like me. We're all the same. Greedy for the happiness of our children. Do you think you are right? So alone. Before there was Salim, too, but now even he has left me.

BABAR: I have to do it.

He puts things into the suitcase.

Have you seen the baby?

MRS RIZVI: Yes, I've seen the pictures.

BABAR: Cute isn't he? You'll be so busy with him, you won't have time to think of me.

MRS RIZVI: How can I forget you even for a minute?

BABAR: Why don't you come and see me off?

MRS RIZVI: Where?

BABAR: At the airport.

MRS RIZVI: No.

BABAR: Come and wish me *'bon voyage'*.

MRS RIZVI: I'll say goodbye to you here.

BABAR: We'll have a bit more time together.

MRS RIZVI: No!

BABAR: Why not?

MRS RIZVI: I can't.

BABAR: What's wrong?

MRS RIZVI: Why, what, when! Please, Babar, don't keep drowning me in questions. I don't want to go.

Pause.

I'll stay here and wait for you. I can feel your presence here, your warmth. I'll keep it with me until you return.

Pause.

Don't go, Babar. Please.

She looks at him, draws him to her. She reads something in Arabic.

SCENE 5

MR RIZVI is sitting on the sofa looking at a newspaper, enjoying it, smiling, laughing occasionally, nodding, making notes.

MR RIZVI: True, very true. 'Innovative ideas…' (*Reads further.*) '…a highly successful textile manufacturing business…' Arrived in England in 1972? It should be 1971. I'll have to make a note of it.

He marks it with the highlighter. MRS RIZVI enters. She begins to dust the furniture.

MR RIZVI: Come, Safia. Come and look at my picture. The gazette has done a victory profile on me. Look, your husband's a famous man.

MRS RIZVI: Go on then.

MRS RIZVI glances at the picture.

Nice. You look…pleased.

MR RIZVI: You think so? Thank you. I was pleased.

MRS RIZVI: Is that today's date?

MR RIZVI: Yes. Would you like to memorize it? The day your husband made his mark on the world. The sixteenth of January, 2002.

He scribbles it on his notepad, tears the sheet off and holds it out to her. She doesn't take it.

MRS RIZVI: Six weeks and two days exactly.

MR RIZVI: Yes, a lot has happened since my campaign began!

MRS RIZVI: Six weeks and two days exactly since he left. And not one word.

He screws the paper up.

MR RIZVI: Safia, you must try not to worry. I know it's difficult. I can't stop thinking about him myself. But I try to keep my mind occupied with other things. You should do the same.

MRS RIZVI: My mind has been occupied. I've been looking at newspapers too, you know. Doing my research. I've been looking into the activities of your party.

MR RIZVI: Really? That's nice. What did you find out?

MRS RIZVI: Lots of things. It's very interesting.

MR RIZVI: It is, isn't it? There's so much we've got planned...

MRS RIZVI: And so much done already. I've collected the clippings.

MR RIZVI: Can I see?

She takes a bundle of papers out of the drawer.

You've been very industrious, Safia. Bring them here. Put them on the table.

She puts them on the table.

Let's have a look.

He reads one.

What's this?

MRS RIZVI: A report of your activities over the last few weeks. Let's see – here you killed two hundred people in a small village.

She grabs another one.

And this? Fifteen people bombed in a hospital. I wonder if that was the treatment they were expecting, lying in their beds. And this one…a family of eight in a house – were they eating their dinner, do you think, when they exploded? I know, I know they were all accidents, of course. Unfortunate for the people involved. What's there to say? Whoops! It's not your fault. And look at this – there's some nice pictures too, of bloodied books and burnt bodies… Here, there's more, more, more, I'll show you lots more, I've kept them all!

She flings the papers at him, then takes more out of the drawers, throwing them everywhere. He tries to stop her but she pushes him off.

MR RIZVI: Safia, please! Stop!

He begins to pick them up.

What have you been doing?

MRS RIZVI: How else could I watch over him?

Pause.

You're so proud to be part of it.

MR RIZVI: No, no, you're wrong. I'm not. You know I've never supported this war, and I've always made my point quite clear. That's all I could do.

MRS RIZVI: You could have resigned. That would have clarified your point. He might have stayed.

MR RIZVI: If you hadn't blessed him he might have stayed.

Silence.

Let's not argue about this now. Instead we should both pray together for his safe return.

They look at each other for a moment, both upset and wanting to reach out, maybe touch the other. SALIM enters. He's carrying a packet of photos.

SALIM: Here you are, Mum – some more pictures of Haroon.

He holds out the photos but she doesn't take them. He puts them on the table.

Have you got it, then?

MR RIZVI gives him the newspaper.

MR RIZVI: It's a bit small, but maybe we can enlarge it on the photocopying machine.

MRS RIZVI: There can't be a machine big enough to fit the size of your head.

SALIM: Why don't you look at the photos, Dad?

MR RIZVI: Yes, I will. Make sure you read it properly. And see if you can spot the mistake.

SALIM: What, this bit you've highlighted?

MR RIZVI: Oh yes, I've already marked it. Never mind.

MR RIZVI starts to look at the pictures.

MR RIZVI: Oh, look at this one! Come and see, Safia. He's a naughty little boy.

She looks at them.

MRS RIZVI: Like granddad? No, he is lovely. Innocent.

MR RIZVI: Yes, Safia, he is like his granddad. Look at him closely – something about the eyes. And the chin. Definitely my chin. I'll have to find my own baby photos.

MRS RIZVI: He looks like Babar. They're his eyes. His chin.

SALIM: Yeah, there is a slight resemblance. There's a bit of me and Lisa too, though, don't you think, Mum?

MRS RIZVI: You, perhaps. I'm not sure I can see anything of her in him.

SALIM: She'd like to come and meet you, if that's alright. Maybe Wednesday?

MR RIZVI: Yes, yes, she's your fiancée, part of the family. She can come and celebrate my victory with us. Isn't that right, Safia? We don't have to worry about other people now.

SALIM: Mum?

MRS RIZVI: Has she read those books I sent her?

SALIM: I don't know if she's had time.

MR RIZVI: What books?

MRS RIZVI: *Signs of the Day of Judgement* and *The Pure and the Punishable.* I thought I would save *Life Beyond the Grave,* and give it to her as a wedding present.

MR RIZVI: Safia, you're unbelievable. You could have waited. Are you trying to scare the poor girl off?

MRS RIZVI: What's wrong with spreading the light of faith? You should read them too. Both of you.

MR RIZVI: I have read them. I don't know how you expect anyone to be illuminated by dark threats and horror stories.

MRS RIZVI: Not everyone is blind to the truth. Anyway, it wasn't my idea. She asked for them. She thinks they might help her fit in.

SALIM: It's true, Dad. Lisa's quite eager to learn and understand about our culture.

MR RIZVI: That's good, that's very good. Just what I like to hear. You should encourage her.

MRS RIZVI: If she decides to become Muslim, then something wonderful will come out of this sorry business. You will stand a chance of being saved too, Salim.

SALIM: I'm not sure she's ready to make any decisions yet, Mum.

MR RIZVI: Of course not. There's no need to force anything on her. It's not conversion that's necessary in this society – it's appreciation. Tolerance of each other.

SALIM: Is Wednesday okay, then?

MRS RIZVI: Will she bring the little one?

SALIM: Of course she will.

MRS RIZVI: Alright. If you must. As long as I can see my little Babar.

SALIM: Haroon, Mum. His name's Haroon.

MRS RIZVI: Yes, I know. Haroon. Haroon. Babar. Haroon.

Pause.

SALIM: I can always take you to see them, if you like.

MRS RIZVI: I'd rather they come here.

SALIM: It might be a nice day out.

MRS RIZVI: I don't want to. If anyone wants to see me, they can come here. I'm here, here, always here. Don't you know that?

SALIM: I was just –

MRS RIZVI: And you – you are always with her now, even after everything, you're not sorry, you don't care, you don't have any shame, you can't wait, you are always with her!

SALIM: What do you want me to do? You never talk to me when I'm here.

Beat.

I'm sorry, Mum.

Pause.

We were hoping to discuss a date for the wedding with you. That'll be better, won't it, Mum? To get everything done properly?

MR RIZVI: There's no need to hurry.

MRS RIZVI: Yes, give them a chance to extend their sin.

MR RIZVI: I just meant…perhaps if you waited…Babar might be back.

MRS RIZVI: Oh. Yes. If you put it that way. It's one of your few good ideas. A very good idea. We must wait for him. Then it will be a true celebration. Maybe he'll surprise us. The end of next month will be good. Set the date for the end of next month.

SALIM: I'll talk to Lisa about it.

MR RIZVI: What do you think, Salim? Shall I keep the whole newspaper, or just cut the article out for my scrapbook? No, not the scrapbook. A frame. One of those fancy gold ones with the scroll patterns. And then we can put it on the wall next to the poster.

He takes the paper over to the wall to see how it looks next to the poster.

You know what this means, don't you? We should be able to start building the youth centre now. The council will have to give us the funds. You see, Safia? How we might finally be able to change something?

The doorbell rings. Exit SALIM.

MRS RIZVI: Youth centre?

MR RIZVI: Yes, a place for our young people. It's important to provide them with a safe recreational environment if we want to keep them off the streets.

MRS RIZVI: A safe place for the young? You are going to provide that?

MR RIZVI: Our children are the future. We must protect them.

MRS RIZVI: You want to protect the children?

MR RIZVI: It's our duty.

MRS RIZVI: But your own child is standing on a battlefield.

Enter AUNTY MOONA and SALIM.

MR RIZVI: Come in, Moona, have you seen my photo? It's a great day for us!

AUNTY MOONA: It is the worst day, Bhai saab.

She takes the paper and puts it to the side without looking at it.

Safia, betho meri behan… [*Sit, my sister…*]

They sit. Lights fade.

SCENE 6

There are white sheets on the floor and a large, smiley photo of BABAR on the wall. On the table is a garland of red roses. MRS RIZVI and AUNTY MOONA are sitting on the floor. They are dressed in white.

MRS RIZVI: The world is full of lies – tongues flipping up and down, twisting, deforming, spewing out sly, horrible nonsense. This must be just another product of an evil mouth.

AUNTY MOONA: You have to believe.

MRS RIZVI: No.

AUNTY MOONA: It has happened.

MRS RIZVI: He will be back.

AUNTY MOONA: Safia, we have solid proof. The building they were in was targeted. The people inside were finished there and then.

MRS RIZVI: No!

AUNTY MOONA: Some of their belongings were found – they sent them back to the mosque.

MRS RIZVI: Where? Let me see.

AUNTY MOONA: I don't advise it.

MRS RIZVI: Show me!

AUNTY MOONA: It will be very difficult.

MRS RIZVI: Just show me, Moona.

AUNTY MOONA holds up a charred bum bag. Then she takes out the towel. MRS RIZVI moves away in shock. Then, after a moment, she grabs it and puts it to her face. AUNTY MOONA leaves her for a minute then tries to pull the towel away from her, but MRS RIZVI resists.

AUNTY MOONA: Chalo, Safia, bas. [*Come, Safia, enough.*]

Pause.

MRS RIZVI: I'll breathe this death into myself.

AUNTY MOONA: Don't say that, Safia. Come on. Just think Babar has got a direct ticket to heaven. That is something rare and special. You must pray now. That will help even more. Come on, give me this.

MRS RIZVI: No, it's all there is.

AUNTY MOONA: Please, Safia. I shouldn't have shown you. I'm going to put it away.

She takes the towel, and gives her some prayer beads.

Take this – and maybe some small comfort will come to you.

She sits her onto the sofa.

Just rest. I'll be back in a minute.

She gathers up the things. Exit AUNTY MOONA. MRS RIZVI starts to whisper something, moving the beads with her fingers. She goes to the drawer and takes out bottles of pills. She takes one and sits on the floor, tipping the tablets out before her. She begins to count them.

MRS RIZVI: One two three four five six seven eight nine ten eleven twelve thirteen fourteen fifteen sixteen seventeen eighteen nineteen twenty twenty-one. Twenty-one. One for each year of his life. Now, what is the best way to take them? All at once?

She gathers them up in her hand and looks at them.

No. They won't all fit in my small and delicate mouth.

Throws them back onto the floor.

Besides, it's bad manners. Two at a time, I think. Nine groups of two and then maybe one of three. Much more ladylike.

She swallows two, with water from a glass on the coffee table. SALIM enters and sits on the sofa. He is wearing a small prayer cap.

SALIM: What are you doing on the floor, Mum? Come and sit here – next to me.

MRS RIZVI: Leave me. I am busy. I am going to see my son.

SALIM: What do you mean?

He crouches down quickly beside her.

Oh my God!

He grabs some of the tablets off the floor.

How many of these have you taken?

MRS RIZVI holds up a tablet to show him.

MRS RIZVI: This is number three. By the time he was three, had memorised all three of his alphabets – English, Arabic, and Urdu. He was a fast learner. That's the problem. Too fast and hot-blooded. That's why he needs me.

She puts the tablet in her mouth and tries to drink water, but he snatches it from her, spilling it over her clothes.

MRS RIZVI: Get off me! Look what you've done, you silly boy! He won't trust me if he thinks I can't even look after myself.

She starts dabbing the water with her shawl.

That's better. Where was I?

She squints at the floor.

Where have they all gone? Did you take them? Give them back! But no. I'll have to get a fresh supply. You've contaminated them with your nasty, dirty hands. I need to be absolutely unstained for this journey.

SALIM: He's gone, Mum. You can't follow him.

MRS RIZVI: Yes I can. You don't know what it is to be faithful, do you? I will follow him.

SALIM: You know this isn't the right way, Mum. It's a sin, isn't it?

She nods.

You want to meet him again, don't you…in paradise?

She nods.

Then promise not to do this again. You must promise me, Mum. Martyrs go to paradise. Suicides don't.

MRS RIZVI: But then – tell me what to do, Salim. What can I do to ease this wrenching, this clawing at my heart? Once you used to help me. You always had the answers. What can I do? To be the mother of a martyr is not enough…

AUNTY MOONA enters, carrying a long piece of silver tinsel.

AUNTY MOONA: Get off the floor, Safia, you will catch cold. Help her up, Salim.

He helps MRS RIZVI onto the sofa.

SALIM: (*To AUNTY MOONA*.) Watch her. Make sure she doesn't get hold of any more pills. I just found her trying to eat the whole bottle.

AUNTY MOONA: This shock is bringing it all out. The depression, the nervousness, the strange thoughts.

SALIM: What are you talking about? Mum's always been mum – a bit paranoid maybe, but…

AUNTY MOONA: Not stepping out further than the garden gate for three years – you call that normal?

SALIM: She goes out.

AUNTY MOONA: Where?

SALIM: I don't know… She goes shopping.

AUNTY MOONA: I do her shopping. Salim, go and phone a doctor, tell him this is an emergency.

SALIM goes out. AUNTY MOONA looks at the rose garland, then puts it back onto the table.

AUNTY MOONA: That is very pretty, that necklace. I could only find this.

She shakes the tinsel and puts it over the picture She sits down on the sofa.

MRS RIZVI: I got the flowers from my garden. I made it myself. I grew them and picked them and wove them together. I often planned how I would make garlands for his wedding.

AUNTY MOONA: Babar was a good boy. Everyone loved him. But maybe Allah loved him more than us, that is why he has taken him. You should be thankful, Safia. Your son had a glorious death. A hero ending.

MRS RIZVI stands up.

MRS RIZVI: Yes, this is where it all ends. Where we are heading from the moment we are born. Each breath takes us nearer. Each breath of pure, life-giving air is just a step closer to the empty grave that awaits us. Do you know who said that?

AUNTY MOONA: Barbara Windsor?

MRS RIZVI: Ali, the great warrior, may Allah be pleased with him. He knew his two sons would be killed. But I didn't know that was all I raised him for. All those years…watching his every move, teaching him, leading him, taking him by the hand…only to bury him, deep, deep, in the ground.

She is walking around the sofa slowly, and breaking the petals off the garland, crushing them with her fingers as she talks. Her hands are stained red with the colour of roses.

But I have been denied even that. I don't even know where he is, where they will put him.

AUNTY MOONA: Try not to think about it. You'll only upset yourself more. I told you, you must try to read dua for him. We will organise a khatam for tomorrow. Everyone will send their blessings to him. Where is Bhai Saab?

MRS RIZVI: How would I know? He's probably noting down last night's adventures in dreamland.

AUNTY MOONA: I didn't know he was interested in dream interpretation.

MRS RIZVI: I'm talking about his naughty nightmares.

She takes out the notebook.

AUNTY MOONA: Safia, I told you to throw that book away. Why have you kept it all these years? You shouldn't hold onto the past like that.

MRS RIZVI: I did throw it away. This is the current version.

AUNTY MOONA: You mean even now he…?

She peeks inside the book.

Chee chee chee chee.

MRS RIZVI: Why? When I tried so hard to clean it, scrub it all away…he keeps bringing it back. Five years of filth to rot away our life. Does he wonder there's not a spot of light in this place? I have never been enough for him.

AUNTY MOONA: Safia, that isn't true.

She takes the book.

This is just fantasy. Bhai saab is coming. Later, you can ask him the reason for these odd urges, but for now, just be nice to each other.

She goes out, as MR RIZVI comes in. He is looking scruffy. He sits on another sofa. He is trying to control himself from crying. They say nothing for a minute.

MR RIZVI: I told him… I told him not to go… He never listened to me. What chance did he have? My brave boy…

MRS RIZVI: He was never your brave boy. You didn't understand what he was trying to do.

MR RIZVI: Stop it, Safia. Why are you saying these things, even now? When we need each other? When nobody else knows how this feels?

MRS RIZVI gets up slowly, and turns to go, but then comes back and kneels down on the floor beside him.

MR RIZVI: You're right. Nobody else knows… It's a beautiful thing we have to share, isn't it? They must have burst him like a balloon… He loved balloons when he was little…those shiny silver ones that rise up and float, free, drifting, all alone. (*Pause.*) Or maybe they shot him. Filled his body with metal. Tore his insides like meat in a mincing machine…

MR RIZVI: Please, Safia…I can't bear it.

He gets up and walks away. He sees the picture and goes up to it, staring. He rips off the tinsel in anger, and tears it into pieces. Then he collapses into tears, on the floor. AUNTY MOONA comes in with a jug of water.

AUNTY MOONA: What are you doing on the floor, Bhai saab, did you fall over? Let me help you.

MRS RIZVI picks up the pieces of tinsel.

MRS RIZVI: Silver and shiny.

AUNTY MOONA: I am very worried about Safia. Her behaviour is not natural.

MR RIZVI: And how would you define natural behaviour?

MRS RIZVI: Free and floating. All alone.

AUNTY MOONA: A normal mother would be crying and wailing, perhaps tearing her clothes. But Safia has kept all the emotion inside.

She thumps her chest.

It is ticking away like a landmine. I have five years' psychology experience.

MR RIZVI: Have you?

AUNTY MOONA: Yes, from watching a very good Indian doctor and sensible agony aunt on *This Morning.*

MRS RIZVI: All alone now. Where are you?

MRS RIZVI puts the tinsel around her neck.

Why can't they find you? Why did this happen to me? I am being punished. I need to be punished.

Wraps the tinsel around her neck tighter. MR RIZVI takes it away from her.

MR RIZVI: What are you doing? Sit down.

She sits down.

MRS RIZVI: I have to cook my keema. Babar likes keema with green peppers. I know what you are going to say. That he's gone and he doesn't need his mother's cooking anymore. But they say even the spirits can smell the aroma of a dish cooked in their name. (*Pause.*) Especially on Thursdays.

MR RIZVI: Leave the keema. You need to rest.

AUNTY MOONA: I will cook dinner today.

MR RIZVI: We must remember that God gives us a better place in the next life. I know your faith is strong, Safia. We'll get through this together, Safia.

MRS RIZVI: Together? Me and you? You and me? Will it help? Will it help me?

MR RIZVI: I don't know… We must try.

MRS RIZVI: Husband and wife, together. It's what we are, after all.

MR RIZVI: That's right.

MRS RIZVI: Shall I tell you something? It's said that one half of your religion is a happy marriage. You have to work at it. Please each other. I should have tried harder. I will make you happy now.

MR RIZVI: Why don't you lie down for a while, or have a hot bath? Put on some fresh clothes?

MRS RIZVI: What is wrong with my clothes?

MR RIZVI: Nothing, nothing is wrong with your clothes. They are just a bit crumpled. You need to look after yourself.

MRS RIZVI: You're right. I should spend more time looking after myself. I will go and do that now.

Exit MRS RIZVI. AUNTY MOONA sits MR RIZVI down.

AUNTY MOONA: See? She doesn't know what she's doing. She needs to see a doctor. She is not coping well at all.

MR RIZVI: She will be alright. She's just confused. The shock was too much for her.

AUNTY MOONA: I don't think you realise it is serious. She just tried to… (*Draws a finger across her throat.*)

MR RIZVI: What?

AUNTY MOONA: She tried to take an overdose of sleeping-pills.

MR RIZVI: You mean she…? Why didn't you tell me?

He gets up to go but she stops him.

AUNTY MOONA: She is looking a little better now. I don't think she will do anything else. Salim is calling the doctor.

MR RIZVI: Still I should check.

AUNTY MOONA: Don't spoil her mood. Anyway, she's gone to the bathroom. You can't watch her every minute.

MR RIZVI: I can't believe Safia tried to…harm herself. I know she's devastated – so am I – but she's always been so sure of herself, so strong.

AUNTY MOONA: Strong?

MR RIZVI: She always has her opinions, you know that. And she has some funny ideas about me. She must have told you.

AUNTY MOONA: Did you ever talk to her about the funny ideas and opinions?

MR RIZVI: Everything she does is so extreme. She only argues with me. I don't have time for it.

AUNTY MOONA: You needed to make time. Perhaps something would have been saved. Perhaps she wouldn't be almost mad.

MR RIZVI: Whenever I tried to tell her about my plans and ideas she wasn't interested. What did you want me to do? There's no point in screaming at a deaf person.

AUNTY MOONA: You have both been deaf to each other. And Safia has been turning strange for a long time. But just think for the future now. You must get her medical attention. I have done what I can – basic analysis. But still I am not a pro.

MR RIZVI: I'll make sure she gets proper help.

AUNTY MOONA: You are a good man. At least deep down you do care. If you ever feel like a cry, my shoulders are always here.

MR RIZVI: I'm alright thank you.

He gets up and begins to tidy the room.

So much mess.

He picks up the tattered garlands.

So many ruined things.

Pause.

AUNTY MOONA: Did you ever find that notebook, Bhai saab?

MR RIZVI: Notebook?

AUNTY MOONA: Didn't you lose your notebook?

MR RIZVI: Oh, yes. I don't know where it is. It must have gone out with the rubbish or something. Why?

AUNTY MOONA: Nothing, nothing. I remember you said it was important, that's why. What was in it? Politician's notes?

MR RIZVI: Er…yes…something like that. It doesn't matter now. Won't your husband be wondering where you are?

AUNTY MOONA: Well, he's got his roti and the teletext is working so I shouldn't think so.

MRS RIZVI steps forward out of the shadows… She is wearing the shiny salwar kameez, that she pulled out of the bag earlier, high heels, and lots of bright make-up, roughly applied. Her hair, which is usually hidden under her scarf, is down, in an attempt at glamour, but is looking messy.

MRS RIZVI: I know how you feel, Moona. Men are difficult to understand, aren't they? I should know. But God likes us to make an effort for our husbands. That's what I did wrong. I was too lazy. But not anymore. What do you think?

She does a twirl. To MR RIZVI.

I know you like attractive women.

Enter SALIM.

89

Come, Salim. You like?

SALIM: It's…

AUNTY MOONA: (*Whispering loudly.*) Humour her, humour her!

SALIM: Very nice.

MRS RIZVI pulls MR RIZVI onto the sofa by the arm. He is horrified by her appearance.

MRS RIZVI: It feels good to be young again. (*To MOONA.*) You should try it. It might work for you too. But it depends. Is Bashir a cheat too? What do they call them, love-rats?

She pokes MR RIZVI in the ribs and giggles.

But not anymore. Things are going to change around here. Now. We need to be free with each other. What do you think, darling?

MR RIZVI: Er…you look lovely.

MRS RIZVI: I'm not quite finished yet, because I know there a few other touches you might like. Let me see… 'One cannot but marvel at the infinite advantages of the push up and plunge…'

MR RIZVI is shocked.

'Smooth contours of almond coloured flesh…a froth of blonde, and gleaming ruby lips offering silent invitations…'

MR RIZVI: Safia! How dare you go through my personal things?

MRS RIZVI: Don't be angry. I'm not. I was upset at first but now I think it's good for me to know what you're really feeling. I'm thinking of going blonde myself. What do you think – platinum or strawberry?

MR RIZVI: You had no right to look at my private...poetry.

MRS RIZVI: Think of it as communication. That's what it's all about. Babar advised me. I will listen to want he says. I don't want him to be angry with me. A good mother, a good wife. Beta, you don't know but your father has a great talent for writing. And he likes sketching too. Where did you put the book, Moona?

MR RIZVI: He doesn't want to see.

SALIM: Yeah, Mum. I think you should leave it.

MRS RIZVI: Then I will recite from it. 'You curve in and out – you are my guitar... I will pluck and strum...'

MR RIZVI: Enough! Safia, please just lie down for a while. You're really not feeling well.

AUNTY MOONA: Haa haa, lie down.

The telephone rings. SALIM goes out to answer it.

It must be another family member offering condolences.

MRS RIZVI: Families, yes, families are very important. A good solid structure is vital. And they are very organic too. Families grow and flourish and spread. (*Pause.*) But my family is shrinking at a very rapid rate.

AUNTY MOONA: Well, you have your little grandson. Your family is growing nicely.

MRS RIZVI: He is lovely, yes. But it's the others. Like him, the one that's just gone out. They get themselves into trouble, and then it's all down to me. Pray, pray, pray. I must pray for their safety, for their health, for them to be forgiven. I spend a lot of hours on my mat. (*To MR RIZVI.*) That's one thing you'll have to understand. I'm a very busy woman. Dressing up smartly like this requires time so we might have to save it for special occasions.

She winks at him, and he looks away. SALIM returns.

SALIM: That was Uncle Qasim. Tariq's father. They've had some news. They've found them – Tariq, Babar, all of them. They're alive.

AUNTY MOONA runs across and hugs SALIM, then MR and MRS RIZVI.

AUNTY MOONA: Hai! Mubarak ho! Mubarak ho! Shukar hai Allah ka! [*Congratulations! Congratulations! Thank Allah!*]

MR RIZVI: Are they sure? What about the reports we had before? They found all their things.

AUNTY MOONA: Yes, what about the forensic evidence?

SALIM: He said they moved a day before, and left a lot of stuff behind. That must have been why there was a mix up. But this time it's definitely them. They're alive.

MR RIZVI: Ya Allah! Thank God! Where are they? What did Qasim say? When are they coming back?

AUNTY MOONA: He's coming home, he's coming home! Chalo, Safia, get ready!

SALIM: No, they won't be back yet.

MR RIZVI: What do you mean they won't? What's happened? Are they alright?

SALIM: Yeah, they're okay.

MR RIZVI: What's the problem then? They have to come back. Babar's had his adventure. It's enough.

SALIM: It's not that easy. They're being held.

MRS RIZVI: Where is he? Is he here?

MR RIZVI: Held? Held by whom?

SALIM: The Allies, I think.

MR RIZVI: But he's British! He can't be captured by his own people. It's probably just a formality.

SALIM: He said something about them being classed as 'high risk'.

MR RIZVI: What? High risk? What rubbish! Give me that phone! I'll talk to someone about this. Don't they know he's my son? He's just a confused boy, not a bloody terrorist.

MRS RIZVI: Bring him to me.

MR RIZVI: Sit down Safia. Don't crowd me. I'm trying to think.

He picks up the telephone.

Who's the best person to call?

SALIM: What about Mr Willoughby?

MR RIZVI: No, I don't think he would understand. His nephew's just joined the RAF.

SALIM: What about that Peter Chadwin-Jones?

MR RIZVI: I wouldn't feel comfortable discussing it with him. It's a delicate issue. Besides, he's already hinted that I used my new position to influence the results of that competition last week. Miss Brent 2002. Of course I didn't. It was just a coincidence that I knew her.

He puts the phone down.

Let's wait a while. See what happens. Maybe it's not as bad as we think. At least we know they're alive. I trust our forces. They'll be kept safe.

SALIM: You have to do something!

MR RIZVI: Yes, but I have to be careful. I can't take advantage of my position. It's unethical. Cheating.

SALIM: Does all that matter now, Dad?

MR RIZVI: Of course it matters. My life's work has been a quest for justice and equality.

MRS RIZVI: You can start again.

MR RIZVI: Don't be ridiculous.

MRS RIZVI: We're making a new start, remember? I will help you. I will learn politics. Just bring him back. You can do it easily.

MR RIZVI: No, I can't.

MRS RIZVI: You said you were a famous man now. Famous people can do what they want.

MR RIZVI: Salim, what exactly did Qasim say?

MRS RIZVI: Everything is easy for you. You're famous. Bring him back.

MR RIZVI: Safia, there are many difficulties, many things I must consider.

MRS RIZVI: None of those things matter. Get my son back. And then later, you'll have me with my new look to keep you busy.

MR RIZVI: (*Shouting.*) What, frigid menopausal homebody turned decrepit old tart?

Silence.

MRS RIZVI: You don't like it.

SALIM: Mum –

MRS RIZVI: Tell me the truth. Do you like my lipstick?

SALIM: Mum!

MRS RIZVI: Do you like my lipstick?

MR RIZVI: No. I don't like it. It's horrible.

SALIM: Dad!

MRS RIZVI: I thought so. In that case I'll show you what justice really is.

She exits.

MR RIZVI: We're lucky to live in this country. We have a very fair system. Babar will be treated with respect.

SALIM: You don't really believe that.

MR RIZVI: But what can I do? Main kya kar sakta hoo? [*What can I do?*] I am only a councillor. What power do I have?

SALIM: You know people. Make some calls. You've got no choice, Dad.

MR RIZVI: He's a fighter. He's got spirit. He'll survive. And he was keen to make sacrifices.

SALIM: So were you. (*Beat.*) You talk about showing the world how wonderful Islam is. You don't remember yourself. At the heart of Islam is the family. Even I know that much. I've spent all this time dividing myself into little pieces so you can all have a bit each. Because I thought you'd do the same for us. I was wrong. I'd do anything for my son.

MR RIZVI: It was all for you. For you, for Babar, yes, and even for Haroon.

SALIM: But it's not what we need, now, at this moment.

MR RIZVI: If I interfere now, it will look like I encouraged him. It will implicate all of us. What will happen then?

SALIM: It can't get any worse.

Beat.

Do you think he would have done it if it wasn't for you?

MR RIZVI: What?

SALIM: He wanted to show you what he could do for himself – but you never see anything, do you? You just wanted him to be another robot. And look what being a good obedient wimp got me. My own father trying to send me into exile, making me hide my son away. I'm pathetic. Mum's always going to hate me, because of what you've done to her.

MR RIZVI: I haven't done…

SALIM: She's been shut up here for God knows how long, her mind spiralling away from anything that makes sense. While you've been partying and giggling and rising up in the world she's plunged into a blackness. But you've been happy, so long as she's been there, doing what she's supposed to, being a wife, with or without a smile on her face. It makes me sick!

He punches the wall.

MR RIZVI: I have been selfish…I'll admit…but never happy… I thought you knew that, Salim… I wasn't happy… The loneliness of being together…it kills you.

SALIM: I thought you believed that everyone has to give something up, compromise somewhere. Otherwise there's only chaos, disaster.

MR RIZVI: Yes… I do…

MRS RIZVI appears, carrying a plastic bag in one hand. The other hand is hidden beneath her shawl. She puts it on the floor in front of MOONA.

AUNTY MOONA: What's in this bag? Presents?

MRS RIZVI: You'll see.

MRS RIZVI walks around behind her husband, grabs him by the neck and puts a knife to his throat.

Stay where you are, everyone.

SALIM: Mum, what are you doing? Let go of him.

MRS RIZVI: Let go? I did let go and look what happened. He's had too much freedom. But I know what must be done. Now, let me see…how well have I taught you all? Who can remember the punishment for a married man who commits adultery?

MR RIZVI: I know. It's stoning to death.

MRS RIZVI: Good boy. And now just take a look at what is inside the bag. Go on, Moona.

AUNTY MOONA looks inside the bag nervously.

Show us all. Not exactly what I would have liked, but they will have to do at such short notice.

AUNTY MOONA holds up a handful of gravel.

AUNTY MOONA: It's those little stones you put in the driveway. I am going to get some of these for my garden. They are good security – very crunchy, so the thief will make too much noise on this –

SALIM: Shut up. Mum, put that knife down please.

MRS RIZVI: Don't talk to your mother like that. Yes, you're right, Moona. They are from our dear future MP's driveway – put there to welcome his new world in. Out with the old, in with the new. And yes, they are an excellent aid for security, a carpet of cosiness, a scattering of safety. But these feelings are unfamiliar to me, so I have thought of other uses. Now, just so that we all understand clearly the course of justice that is taking place here today – we have established this man is an adulterer –

MR RIZVI: How? Where is your proof?

MRS RIZVI gets angry and yanks his hair. He moans.

MRS RIZVI: You just keep quiet. We're not asking you.

SALIM: But he's right. You need four eyewitnesses to the act before you can proceed any further – you can't just twist the law to suit you.

MRS RIZVI: Oh, but bending rules is very much in fashion. Everybody's doing it – soldiers heroes priests presidents. (*Beat.*) I'm lucky – I have no need for trivial points and petty regulations. My life's been made easy by a full confession.

MR RIZVI: What confession?

She smacks him.

MRS RIZVI: Look, I'm in charge here, and I know he's guilty.

She takes out the notebook.

Exhibit number one. It's all in here, every little detail of what he's been up to. It does belong to you, doesn't it?

MR RIZVI: Yes.

MRS RIZVI: And this is your writing?

MR RIZVI: Yes, but –

MRS RIZVI: Want me to read some more out?

MR RIZVI: No, don't.

MRS RIZVI: Guilty on the first charge, then.

MR RIZVI: But none of it's true, Safia. I made it all up. I was bored so I wrote a few…jokes.

MRS RIZVI: And to the charge already mentioned you might add the crime of desertion. The worst type of betrayal possible. The desertion of a son by his father. (*Pause.*) Now, I want you all to pick up some stones and throw them at the prisoner. Come on, chop chop. We haven't got all day.

Nobody moves, so she presses the knife menacingly on his throat.

Or shall I just finish him off myself?

They slowly pick up handfuls of gravel, and throw it feebly at MR RIZVI. Most of them land on the sofa, except for AUNTY MOONA's, which are better aimed and thrown with more force, hitting him in the stomach.

Is that the best you can do? Harder, please, or we'll be here all week. You know, when you were out with your famous friends and ministers I was busy trying to keep the weeds away. I found them very stubborn. Take the big ones out too. I put a few rocks in for good measure.

They are both on the floor, rummaging through the bag. Only AUNTY MOONA takes out a big stone. MRS RIZVI smiles.

Aim for the head.

MR RIZVI: Safia, why are you doing this? I promise you, I've done nothing. I love you.

MRS RIZVI: That's something I haven't heard you say for about ten years. Not to me anyway. And how I've longed for it.

She puts her face to his ear.

Desperate men make lousy liars.

MR RIZVI: It's the truth.

She jabs hard at his chest with the handle of the knife.

What would Babar say if he could see you now?

MRS RIZVI: Babar? Where is he? You told me he was gone. You said you wouldn't bring him back.

MR RIZVI: I'll bring him back. He's coming.

MRS RIZVI looks up at the ceiling, as if searching for him. SALIM quickly lunges forward and tries to take the knife. They struggle slightly and she cuts his hand. She drops the knife and begins to wrap his hand with her dupatta. She looks at her hand, which has his blood on it.

MRS RIZVI: I'm sorry... I'm so sorry.

She starts crying. SALIM hugs her.

SALIM: It's alright. Everything's alright. (*Beat.*) Are you okay, Dad?

AUNTY MOONA: Shall I get an elastoplast?

MR RIZVI: Just leave.

Exit AUNTY MOONA. MR RIZVI takes down his poster and begins to roll it. Blackout.

End.

BELLS

Characters

MADAM

53 years old. Manages the club as well as managing the dancers. Born and brought up in Lahore, Pakistan. Well dressed in cream or white shalvar Kameez suits all the time. She wears gold jewellery and smokes a water and tobacco bong (hookah) and drinks tea from a flask and a plastic beaker. She is a practising Muslim.

AIESHA

20 years old, dancer. Born and brought up in Pakistan. Wears glamorous tight fitting shalvar kameez suits, loads of make-up and jewellery. Doesn't smoke but drinks whisky. She is a practising Muslim.

CHARLES

35 years old. British Indian, middle class accountant. Born and brought up in Cambridgeshire. Now working in London. Smokes and drinks wine. Wears smart but casual-looking business suits, silk ties and has a smart leather rucksack with him at all times. Wears a gold watch and a gold ring on his little finger. And has trendy spectacles.

PEPSI

27 years old, transvestite. Born and brought up in London, is from an Indian Sikh parentage. Wears fitted bootleg trousers, fitted t-shirts with logos printed on them and funky trainers. He has long hair tied in a ponytail or plait. During the day he wears light make-up and for the club nights he wears female dress and loads of make-up and jewellery. Doesn't smoke. Drinks and sniffs poppers.

ASHRAF

55 years old. Owner of the butcher's shop and the club above. Balding with thick rimmed spectacles; wears shirt and trousers that look as if they're from the sixties. When he's in the shop he has a white blood-stained apron on. He loves to keep his shop clean and tidy.

CUSTOMERS

BELLS

The play is set in a south Asian courtesan club that is above a butcher's shop in east central London. The audience is to be treated as club members. Before the performance each member of the audience is given a wad of fake money which they can spend if they wish at Bells during the dance performances.

½lb Lamb's Heart

Opening scene – summertime. Rain outside and sounds of cars driving in rain. Windows open with soft breeze coming in.

A melodic Islamic call for prayer plays on a broken decorative Azan [call for prayer] *clock which is part of the set.*

Lights vary from ASHRAF (who is in the butcher's shop), MADAM and AIESHA.

ASHRAF, MADAM and AIESHA are all occupied reading Namaz [prayer]. *They're at various stages of either having read Namaz or folding up their prayer mats, to being completely absorbed in prayer. But everyone is silent as prayer times are the rare moments of tranquillity at Bells. There is some slight interaction between characters when they're not reading Namaz but this is just merely to pass a book to each other or to shove up on the sofa.*

Both AIESHA and MADAM have their heads covered with their dupatta [scarves] *and ASHRAF is wearing a prayer hat. PEPSI is lying down with his headphones on listening to his music and reading a magazine. The three finish Namaz and fold up their mats.*

1lb Mince

Set in the butcher's shop, which has a small amount of other groceries and confectionery.

ASHRAF is cleaning the shop floor and preparing for the shop to be closed. There is an Asian radio station playing in the background. MADAM is sitting to the side of the counter with her flask of tea, sipping away. She is very stern and serious, however she does let out the occasional smile. She is listening to ASHRAF and also has an eye constantly wandering around the shop floor surveying customers. MADAM has a tight-fitting shalvar kameez [trouser and tunic] *suit on in white with a low cleavage and very slinky, sparkly two-inch heeled sandals. Her hands are decorated with henna, and her hair is dyed orangey red with henna. She has very little make-up on and always wears a veil softly on her head. ASHRAF is wearing his butcher's apron, big white trainers and a floral shirt with black trousers.*

PEPSI and AIESHA walk into ASHRAF's butcher's shop laden with shopping bags, joking and laughing. PEPSI is dressed in a pair of jeans, trainers and T-shirt and AIESHA is wearing simple cotton shalvar kameez suit and flat thong sandals, no make-up and her hair tied in a bun. They waltz into the shop and start filling their pockets with goodies that take their fancy as they make their way through the shop to go upstairs to Bells.

PEPSI: We so should have got that pink suit. It was so cool.

AIESHA: Is it cool we want – or is it hot?

PEPSI & AIESHA: Hot! Hot! Hot!

ASHRAF: Have you two been shopping again?

PEPSI: Yes we've brought loads of goodies.

MADAM: How much did you spend?

PEPSI: Just £150.

AIESHA: (*Rummaging in her bags to show them.*) We got two suits and a new nose stud for me.

MADAM: Did you go to the goldsmiths and ask him to fix my Rani Haar? [*queen necklace*].

PEPSI: Yes he said he's got a shipment coming in from Pakistan, with pearls that will match your necklace.

AIESHA: So it'll take two weeks to fix.

MADAM: Two weeks!

ASHRAF: (*Sarcastically.*) Only two weeks?

MADAM: In Pakistan I used to get the designer to design, the goldsmith to make, and the servants to pick up my jewellery all on the same day. What is this country like?

ASHRAF: Anyway you two, you're late!

MADAM: Why did you take so long?

AIESHA: I... I...was looking for a...a dupatta [*scarf*] to match that gold...

PEPSI: ...outfit of yours.

MADAM: Oh yes you good girl. So...where is it, let me see?

PEPSI: Ahhhh! Well! We couldn't quite get the match.

MADAM: Ugh you bloody time wasters...get upstairs and start sorting yourselves out for this evening.

ASHRAF: Go on, off you go, what you standing around here making my shop look untidy.

ASHRAF playfully throws a wet dishcloth at them, which hits PEPSI.

Giggling, AIESHA and PEPSI walk off stage.

MADAM gives ASHRAF an irritated look and reluctantly picks up the dishcloth.

MADAM: I really wanted to wear that suit tonight. (*Pause.*) I think Mr Shah is coming to visit me this evening.

ASHRAF ignores her. Pause.

ASHRAF: Last night I saw…the little short one from Heera Mandi. The one with the stutter. Oh you know… Do you remember when we used to go for a walk near the Shahi Musjid [*royal Mosque*] and he used to come to us, trying to get me to buy a rose for you. (*Laughs.*) You only wanted fresh Jasmine for your hair.

MADAM: (*Uninterested.*) Oh Sufi Gulab [*Sufi rose*].

ASHRAF: Yes, yes…good name you gave him… Sufi Gulab.

MADAM: He was a right clown. With his wiry beard…

ASHRAF: Well he hasn't changed.

ASHRAF wanders off into the back room and comes out again.

Wearing a screwed up old shirt and trousers that were too short for him.

MADAM: Some people have no class.

ASHRAF: What a mover in society. Vah!

MADAM: How the hell did he manage to get to England?

ASHRAF: He was saying something to me about he got married to a cousin?

MADAM: No really?

ASHRAF: She's a cripple and so her family didn't mind her having him for a husband.

MADAM: Bastards! The things our people put their children through for the sake of bastard bloody honour and money. Lalchy logue [*Greedy people*].

ASHRAF: That is why the English are very civilised in the their own way.

ASHRAF is clearing up and MADAM is counting the till money with precision and elegance.

MADAM: Maybe the English are, but we have much better family values. We can easily tell the good people, from the bad people. The English are so uptight and reserved; you never know what they are thinking inside.

ASHRAF: If you're going to compare, then the average English man behaves…like the upper classes in Pakistan. That's still something worth appreciating.

MADAM: Maybe…to hell with them all…

She finishes counting the money.

That's all counted…

MADAM pulls at ASHRAF's apron in a seductive manner and signals him to give her a kiss.

ASHRAF ignores her signals and carries on working.

MADAM is annoyed and feels rejected.

Don't you love me any more? We've been together so long that we're like brother and sister.

ASHRAF: Oh don't start all that again. Why worry about love…love is just a word. Meri jaan. Look at me. There is no woman in the world that can replace you.

MADAM: A feminist! It doesn't suit you.

ASHRAF: But you suit me.

He squeezes her cheeks lovingly.

MADAM: (*Giggles.*) Get off you silly old fool. Tell me about Sufi Gulab… Shaukat. What happened?

ASHRAF: Oh god, that bloody fool? Where did I get up to?

MADAM: He has married his crippled cousin.

ASHRAF: Oh yes. Bloody idiot was standing around last night and wouldn't leave. Making the place look messy and cheap. He says: 'Ashraf Saab, soonia hai [*heard*] you have a very good club here. I hear it is theatre type thing. Good music-shousic, drink-shink and good dancers.' Bloody fool.

MADAM: 'Drink-shrink'?

ASHRAF: I said 'Shaukat Ji this is a members club, it costs a lot of money to join'.

MADAM: His face must have sunk.

ASHRAF: No, no, no. (*Quotes.*) 'I'm not that poor flower boy you once knew. We both come from the same gutters'… (*Talking to himself.*) What did Mrs Kaur say, four pounds or five?

MADAM: Ugh!

ASHRAF: I got angry and I asked the bouncers to tell him puck off, ma yuddah bastard!

MADAM: Did he go?

ASHRAF: 'Did he go?' Of course he didn't. Shouting 'you pimp, you eunuch, kaffir [*devil worshipper*]. I'm going to tell everyone at the Masjid about you.'

MADAM: Let him tell the world.

ASHRAF: (*Talking to himself.*) Is that all? Okay. That's £9.54…

He writes the price on the bag of meat with a thick blue marker.

MADAM: Our paperwork is in excellent order, everything is above board… Isn't it? We have nothing to worry about?

ASHRAF: Yes of course the papers are okay. Low lifes, kya? Whatever we do has to be illegal hah?

MADAM: Jealousy.

ASHRAF: He said he's going to tell Zenab…

MADAM: You told him you divorced her?

ASHRAF: But she is the mother of my daughter.

MADAM: You've been sending her a money order every month. She's not your wife any more.

ASHRAF sighs.

ASHRAF: Meri jaan it's Shamsa she'll be a young woman soon. It's not a pretty world out there.

MADAM: She'll do just fine. She could always live here with us.

ASHRAF: (*Slamming his cleaver down.*) Shut up. Don't ever say that to me again. I keep you like a queen. Don't I?

ASHRAF goes to lock the shop door.

Here comes one of our lovely regular ulloos [*idiots*].

CHARLES rushes in pleading on his mobile phone and miming to ASHRAF to let him into the shop even though it's too late.

ASHRAF agrees busily.

CHARLES is dressed in a cream linen suit with a bright silk tie and a smart briefcase. He browses around as he talks. He constantly combs his hair with his fingers or just shakes his head to flick his fringe away from his eyes.

Sorry we're closing… (tut) okay then.

MADAM: Buukwaas [*What rubbish*]. Go talk to your dark Indian, I mean English gentleman.

CHARLES: (*To ASHRAF.*) Thank you, thank you. (*Back to phone call.*) I'll pick up some steak; I'm at the halaal butcher's shop…and an excellent claret…yes…but…sweetheart…

ASHRAF: You see what a gentleman?

MADAM: He has to be…because that is how he was brought up. Anyway he's one of us?

ASHRAF: Yes of course he is one of us but also…well…nooo…nooo he's English…brown English.

MADAM: Then that explains it…if he's English then he doesn't know anything else, but to do mous mous [*sniff sniff*] around women.

CHARLES is in the background shopping and chatting on the phone.

MADAM and ASHRAF are talking to each other and listening in on CHARLES.

MADAM pours a cup of tea out of her flask and begins to sip it slowly.

What is Claret anyway?

ASHRAF: It's a wine, must be a bloody good one because he seems to be showing off. Why not just say wine? Must be like Blue Nun, Claret huh?

MADAM: What a cheap trick. Give her some gold or diamonds. Wine is just urine, in one end and out the other.

CHARLES: It's fine, really it's fine. I understand. I've got heaps of paperwork to do, anyway. Enjoy yourself on your girlie night out.

CHARLES hangs up, puts the empty shopping basket back and starts to leave the shop feeling very sad.

Bye, bye. (*Waves to ASHRAF.*)

ASHRAF: Oh you not buying anything today sir?

CHARLES: No thanks, my date has just cancelled on me.

ASHRAF: Oh dear sir. I'm sorry. You could still take a piece of steak? Claret sounds like a very special bottle?

CHARLES: Oh you heard?

ASHRAF: Oh sir I wasn't listening in, it was just that I was sad to see you looking so unhappy.

CHARLES: Yes well it's probably my own fault.

ASHRAF: No, no, no you seem to me the perfect gentleman. It is the ladies; they like to keep us on our toes.

CHARLES: I couldn't be more on my toes if I tried. I'd be looking like a ballerina soon… I'll…

MADAM: You like ballet?

CHARLES: Well yes I do…sort of, but it was really meant as an analogy.

MADAM: So you like dance sir?

CHARLES: Yes.

MADAM: Very good, very good. Now don't be too upset about girlfriends. You are young and very handsome. There must be plenty of ladies after you?

CHARLES: (*Embarrassed laugh.*) Thank you… But, well I can't be left on the shelf for much longer or else I'll die a lonely old man.

MADAM: No, no you mustn't say that. Tobah! Tobah! [*Heaven forbid!*]

CHARLES: Ashraf your wife's kind and beautiful. You're a lucky man.

MADAM blushes and smiles.

ASHRAF: Thank you sir, I am a very blessed man, indeed.

MADAM: I'm not as beautiful as I used to be, you know. I used to have men falling at my feet when I was younger.

CHARLES: I can believe that. It's a shame you don't have a sister for me.

MADAM: Oh you charmer. Come here and let me look at your hand.

CHARLES: Sorry?

MADAM: Come on, just come over to me and show me your hand.

ASHRAF: Madam please, leave the poor boy alone?

MADAM: You be quiet and get on with your work.

CHARLES goes over to MADAM and shows her his palm. She looks at it in a very informed manner. CHARLES is slightly embarrassed but also curious.

Hucha [*Right*] ...hum...hum...ooow...

ASHRAF: Ignore her sir; she thinks she can tell the future.

CHARLES: Well what can you see? Go on tell...

MADAM: Do you believe?

CHARLES: No...but I am curious.

MADAM: Well if you don't believe then it's a waste of time. Do you believe?

CHARLES: umm...ahhhhh...yes I do believe.

MADAM: Right, well this is your lifeline. And to me it looks... (*Seductively.*) very long. And...squeeze your palm...yes that's it...that is how many children you're going to have…vah you saucy boy…there are three lines here…you're going to have three children…

ASHRAF: (*Waving and shouting out across the street to someone.*) I'll have the Halal burgers in next week. Sorry.

CHARLES: Don't know how, I haven't had a girlfriend! About two years now.

MADAM: Well it doesn't all dry up down there, you know! You're young yet, not like my poor Ashraf.

ASHRAF: Aye there's plenty of life in this tiger yet.

MADAM: What's the use of a tiger with no teeth and claws?

ASHRAF waves his meat cleaver.

ASHRAF: But darling don't be fooled by my looks. I have the biggest chopper in London.

CHARLES: Easy tiger!

ASHRAF waves his chopper about recklessly.

CHARLES laughs but is nervous of the cleaver.

Steady on… (*He winks at ASHRAF.*) Ladies present and all that.

MADAM: Ooh look there are breaks in this line, which must be some sort of change in your life or maybe a journey.

CHARLES: Can't be a journey. I've just been away for the whole of the summer. Went to tour India on a 'roots and culture' type trip. Lovely it was. Beautiful beaches and beautiful people.

ASHRAF: Not as beautiful as the Pakistanis.

CHARLES: Well… I wouldn't quite compare…

MADAM: You have lovely hands and a good future ahead of you. I say, be strong and follow your path.

CHARLES: Well my lovely lady, my path at this moment is home with a bag of chips and then bed with a good book.

ASHRAF looks over to MADAM for agreement.

ASHRAF: Oh sir you should stay and have dinner with us tonight.

CHARLES: Ashraf thank you but I must say no. But it's very kind of you to offer.

ASHRAF: It's no trouble.

CHARLES: Anyway, you must have your hands full, what with managing two businesses. I don't know how you do it.

ASHRAF: Well Madam manages the members' club and I manage the shop.

MADAM: It's simple really. One's open during the day and the other at night.

CHARLES: Great stuff. You seem rather well organised. (*Awkward.*) I'm off now.

ASHRAF: Sure you won't stay sir?

MADAM: And remember you have three babies to make.

CHARLES: Oh for goodness sake. Listen Ashraf, please stop calling me sir. I feel you know me and yet you never use my name.

ASHRAF: No, no sir it's rude. You're a big important man.

CHARLES: I'm Charles and for God's sake Ashraf, I'm a pathetic loser who happens to have been born into the right sort of family. I'm no more important than any other man.

MADAM: What do you mean the right sort of family? Are you suggesting that we haven't?

CHARLES: God no! Bloody hell, you see what an idiot I am. I meant the sort of family that put up with all my stupid failures in life. I feel I'm never good enough. Well, my mother puts up with me but father sometimes has other views.

ASHRAF: Mothers vah! Yes, yes sir I know what you mean…

CHARLES: Charles. Please.

ASHRAF: Sorry Charles.

CHARLES: I think I may have upset your lovely wife?

MADAM: No, no I'm not upset. Charles… I was just thinking what different worlds we live in.

ASHRAF: Oh no, she's going to get into one of her philosophical moods.

CHARLES: I don't think it's that different.

MADAM: Charles, why don't you come along to our entertainment club upstairs? I think you'll like it.

CHARLES: I'm not really a club type guy.

ASHRAF: No my darling, I think Charles isn't wanting to come to our entertainment club.

CHARLES: What do you mean Ashraf? If your lovely wife thinks I might like it then yes I will at least consider it. Thank you. I've actually been introduced to a few Bollywood films…and of course I know where to shop for the best spices – (*Meaning ASHRAF's shop.*) The posters outside for your club look very colourful and may I add…exotic.

MADAM and ASHRAF both smile at CHARLES to acknowledge what he's saying but ASHRAF is now unsure.

ASHRAF: But darling I don't think…

MADAM: Shush you.

CHARLES: I'm getting to know quite a lot about my cultural history these days.

ASHRAF: Charles I really don't…

CHARLES: (*Cutting in.*) *Dharam Veer* and *Kabi… Kabi…* great films. Shush Ashraf. (*Laughs.*)

MADAM: Shush… I run the club and I know that Charles will like it. (*She smiles.*)

ASHRAF: Darling…but…

MADAM: Listen to me Charles. Do you like music?

CHARLES: Yes. Yes I'm very much into all these new music fusions with world sounds.

MADAM: Do you like good food?

CHARLES: Yes of course.

ASHRAF: No food at the club.

MADAM: Do you like pretty girls or pretty boys?

CHARLES: Wow…pretty girls of course. None of my business what pretty boys get up to but it's not for me.

MADAM: Okay…then I think an evening at Bells should make a new man out of you. Our own Pakistani Heera Mandi in London.

CHARLES: What's that…Heera Mandi???

MADAM: You'll see.

CHARLES: You're promising an awful lot.

MADAM: I've been in the entertainment business since I was fourteen and I can tell a lot about a man and what he might want on a Friday night.

CHARLES: You mean tonight? Don't you have to be a member?

ASHRAF: Yes but tonight you can be our guest, first see if you enjoy it, then become a member.

CHARLES: I've always wondered about Bells.

MADAM pours more tea.

MADAM: We won't be open until 10pm but please do come along.

CHARLES: Thank you, I will…actually… I'll think about it.

CHARLES exits.

ASHRAF: What a gentleman.

MADAM: Yes I wish you could be like him sometimes.

ASHRAF: My darling, meri jaan [*my life*] if every time you smiled and rose petals fell out of your mouth then maybe I would be a gentleman but instead I get sour lemon smiles from you. Now where's the justice in that?

MADAM: You need lemons to break up all the treacle that's clogging up your tiny brain!

ASHRAF: Baby. My tiny brain is the magic behind our success. You love me and I love you.

2lbs Steak

Set in one of the bedrooms at Bells. AIESHA is in a towel, grooming herself with perfumes and oils. PEPSI is also in a towel, sitting holding a hand mirror plucking his eyebrows. Funky Lollywood tunes are playing in the background. They are both giggling and singing along to the music, acting out the words. AIESHA is practising her dance routines.

PEPSI & AIESHA: Tenu sajde karan noon jee kar da pir sooch di ah tu khuda te nahee. [*I feel like bowing down at worshipping you but then I think you're not God.*] Teray baj marun nu jee kar da, pir sooch di ah tu jooda te nahee. [*I feel like dying in your arms but then I think maybe you're too distant for me.*]

PEPSI: No, no jump up a bit more. Shake your tits. Look like this.

AIESHA: I was.

PEPSI: Move your hips and make me want to fuck you.

AIESHA: Jaani I'm good but not that good. I doubt that I'll ever be able make you want to fuck me.

PEPSI: Miracles have happened before.

AIESHA: Aye a miracle happens here every night.

PEPSI: Yes and we create those miracles.

AIESHA: (*Sarcastically.*) Now, now it's not just us creating miracles. Madam does her fair share too.

PEPSI: The only miracle she performs is with the dregs at the end of the night.

AIESHA: Hey those dregs, they feel they're getting a bargain and she feels like she's a wanted woman.

PEPSI: Pppfff! What you wearing tonight?

AIESHA: Don't know yet.

PEPSI: I think…a boob tube number.

AIESHA: Ooh I say Jaani.

PEPSI: I'm gonna put that new belly ring in that we bought today. Talking of today, when we're out shopping, you can stop all this bumping into blokes…customers…and chatting rubbish. I'm supposed to be keeping an eye on you, don't make life difficult.

AIESHA: (*Ignoring him.*) Belly ring…well in that case, Jaani, you should wax your belly 'cos that won't do!

PEPSI: Do you think it's that hairy? I thought I might get away with it.

AIESHA: Did you now?

She pushes him softly.

Lie back.

PEPSI: I know what you were up to today.

AIESHA: What?

PEPSI: Well…when we're out, don't try to sneak off.

AIESHA brings over the wax strips, gets PEPSI to lay down and she starts to wax around his belly and hips.

Aaaaaahhhhhhhhh! Fuck!

AIESHA: Pepsi Jaani when was the last time you got your bikini line done?

PEPSI: Couple of weeks ago…aaaaahhhhhhhhh! Man! Can't you be gentle!

AIESHA: Like hell you did. These bastards are creeping up thick and fast. Better be careful before your little soldier gets all tangled up in there. You won't be able to pee let alone do anything else.

PEPSI: Yuck shut up. You're gross. Sssssiiiiiiiiii! Aaaahhhhh! Si! I'll go shopping without you, you know…and I'll choose your outfits.

She examines his navel closer and then grabs the tweezers off him and starts to pluck hairs that she might have missed.

AIESHA: Really?

PEPSI: Ouch! Ooooh! Ouch! Be careful don't pull my knob off.

AIESHA: I'll try not to. But I can't even see it at the moment.

PEPSI: That's 'cos it's not for you to look at.

AIESHA: Excuse me.

PEPSI: Well girlfriend my meat is destined for higher things in life.

AIESHA: What, Ashraf's shitty bottom? Here you're done!

PEPSI: (*Sarcastically.*) Cheers girlfriend...my Ashraf's bottom is as juicy and soft as a peach.

AIESHA: You mean a shrivelled peach. What do you see in him?

They both start to put on their make-up.

PEPSI: (*Pointing the mirror at his navel.*) What do you mean?

AIESHA: You know what I mean.

PEPSI: I love him.

AIESHA: A dirty old man?

PEPSI: No different to the dirty old men you shag.

AIESHA: Yes but I'm not in love with them.

PEPSI: You've got a rock not a heart.

AIESHA: Ooh listen to you...all high and mighty!

PEPSI: Look I might not be into books and things like you, but I know a good thing.

AIESHA: Tell me Pepsi, what's a good thing?

PEPSI: You know what I mean!

PEPSI takes off his towel to put on his corset, whilst carefully tucking his penis back and starts to put on a strapless bra stuffed with silicone gel pads to give him a cleavage.

Like my body for instance. (*Laughs.*) That's a good thing!

AIESHA: No I don't know what you mean…a good thing?! Come here let me sort your corset out. Tuck your soldier in a bit more, I can see a slight lump.

PEPSI: Oops!

AIESHA: So what do you mean 'a good thing'?

PEPSI: Listen, let's chat when you're not so close to my dick?

AIESHA: Why you worried that I might turn you on?

PEPSI: No!

AIESHA: Don't you trust me?

PEPSI: Yeah I do.

AIESHA: What is it then?

PEPSI: What do you mean?

AIESHA: Why is it you jump up whenever Madam or Ashraf click their fingers?

AIESHA starts taking off her towel and starts to get dressed by putting on sexy underwear and a gloriously sequinned and embroidery Langah [long flowing skirt] *with a tight fitting sari blouse.*

PEPSI and AIESHA help each other get dressed.

PEPSI: No I don't.

AIESHA: Yes…we can all live in denial.

PEPSI: I'm not the one in denial.

AIESHA: Really?

PEPSI: You think you're too high and mighty. Ashraf makes me feel real. I can be who I am with him. I don't have to pretend.

AIESHA: 'Course you do. Look at you. If that isn't pretence then what is?

PEPSI: I tell you this is a performance. Just like you perform.

AIESHA: Let's not argue…there's better out there for us.

PEPSI: Just because you've been with Madam since you were thirteen doesn't mean you've missed out on anything.

AIESHA: Haven't I?

PEPSI: I've been out there and the world is a bastard to the likes of you and me. Really it is.

AIESHA: I'm not like you.

PEPSI: You are to the world.

AIESHA: What world? The world of 'Bells', or the world of humans?

PEPSI: Do you really think anyone's gonna believe that you're an educated Pathan from Peshawar or a two-bit whore who chose this profession?

ASHRAF walks in without knocking. He has a carrier bag full of books.

ASHRAF: What you two bitches whining on about?

PEPSI: (*Sarcastically.*) Knock! Knock!

AIESHA: This profession.

ASHRAF: (*Eyeing her up in an indecent manner.*) Aieshee, when will you learn to accept. Your parents didn't want you darling. We're your family. This profession is built on the misfortunes of lovely girls like you. (*He squeezes her cheeks.*) We are Kanjar [*caste which undertakes prostitution as their traditional family occupation*] and you're a kanjari [*feminine of kanjar*].

PEPSI: (*Rushing to ASHRAF and flirting in an extremely feminine way.*) Oh let's talk about something cheery.

AIESHA: I suppose you don't have any influence on our misfortunes?

ASHRAF grabs AIESHA's hair and allows his hand to casually sweep over her breast.

ASHRAF: Here we go again. Of course we do have influences, that's why you're here and not in some Pakistani gutter being fucked by homeless rats.

PEPSI: Okay, okay, Ashraf darling let's not go there boo boo? (*Grabs him and gives him a lustful kiss.*)

ASHRAF: (*To PEPSI.*) Oh Rani [*queen*] control yourself. Not in front of our delicate flower.

ASHRAF traces his finger along AIESHA's back.

PEPSI: Aren't I a delicate flower?

ASHRAF: You my Rani are a rose. A perfect Indian Rose. Any Sikh would be proud to have you stuck in his Pug [*turban*].

PEPSI: What about a naughty Muslim like you?

ASHRAF: Rani. Allah knows I'm your slave.

PEPSI: Oh stop it, you're just teasing. Say 'sau guru di' [*I swear by Guru*].

ASHRAF: Sau Guru di, Allah Ki Kasam [*I swear by Allah*] and Kali Mah ki sau [*I swear by Kali Mah*]. And I swear by Jesus Christ. Are you happy now?

AIESHA: (*She laughs.*) You two are so silly.

MADAM walks in all made up and dressed in her silks and finery. She's trying to fasten a piece of jewellery and without asking indicates to AIESHA to fasten it up. She strokes AIESHA on the head as if she's blessing her.

MADAM: Come on hurry up it's late. What are you all laughing about?

ASHRAF: Meri Jaan we're laughing at the moon, we're laughing at the stars, we're laughing at this mysterious night and what he'll bring to our hearts.

MADAM: Ashraf I do wish you'd stop living on the moon and join the real world sometimes.

ASHRAF: The real world is full of darkness and pain.

MADAM: Aieshee darling you look beautiful.

PEPSI: She does, doesn't she?

MADAM: And you, Ashraf's little Rani, is that a lovely stomach or is it a work of art?

ASHRAF grabs PEPSI and lovingly kisses his stomach like a hungry savage.

PEPSI giggles.

Come on, come on, the staff are already here. I think we're going to be blessed with some real gentlemen tonight. So you two better be on form.

She drinks some more tea from her flask.

ASHRAF: I have a little something for you all. Aieshee, your books, the second-hand bookshop woman suggested these.

AIESHA: Oh thank you Ashraf Ji.

ASHRAF: I tell you, that woman at the bookshop thinks I am so well read; she keeps flirting with me and asking my opinion on the books. She doesn't know what I really think to all this bloody reading for fun shit…

AIESHA starts skim-reading the books.

And you, meri jaan, some sweet paan.

MADAM: (*She peers inside.*) Wow there's enough here for the whole weekend.

PEPSI: What about me?

ASHRAF: How can I forget you? It came through the post today. Here the latest *Breasts'r'Us* magazine. We can both choose a pair of new breasts for you. Nothing too big. A handful is just enough.

PEPSI: (*Flicking through the pages quickly.*) Wicked. Have they got a sale on yet?

MADAM: Aiesha put those books down and go and get something to eat.

ASHRAF: I don't want you passing out because you haven't eaten!

MADAM: And can both of you take it easy on the booze tonight.

ASHRAF: We're supposed to be making a profit.

MADAM: Pepsi you drink more than you earn!

PEPSI: That's not fair!

MADAM: Well it's true.

ASHRAF: Okay, okay never mind. Go on, off you go.

MADAM tries to fondle ASHRAF but he doesn't seem to react.

Leave me alone woman, I've got some work to do.

MADAM: You're not the only one.

MADAM storms off to another part of the stage to count the takings. This is not a conventional office but more a sort of sitting room/bedroom.

ASHRAF lies back and starts to read Breasts'r'Us *magazine.*

MADAM is sorting through some paperwork and counting the takings from the black bag which is always on stage during the club nights. MADAM keeps this bag, which is a bit like a small black sports bag, during the club nights. In it PEPSI and AIESHA collect money which is bestowed upon them from appreciative customers during their dances. AIESHA and PEPSI, having collected the money, play about with it seductively, but then eventually put it into this bag.

ASHRAF: It's amazing!

MADAM: What?

ASHRAF: Modern technology.

MADAM: What are you talking about?

ASHRAF: You get all sorts of shapes and sizes…

MADAM: Um huh?

ASHRAF: There's round ones, long ones, lop-sided ones.

MADAM: A bit like your ears…lop-sided.

ASHRAF: Wow to have a sense of humour… There's some here that look like something that's on my chopping board. You haven't been posing for this have you? They look just like your boobies.

MADAM: (*Laughs.*) Shut up, good for nothing dhanger [*ass*].

She throws a book at him.

Get up and do something useful.

ASHRAF: What do you want me to do? I've been on my feet all day.

MADAM: I need you to sort out all those membership forms. The girl at the door is useless.

MADAM continues cashing up what is in the black bag.

ASHRAF: Why don't you bloody well do it, you seem to be sitting on your rump steak all day?

MADAM: Oh I suppose I do nothing, do I?

ASHRAF: Well…you always blame everyone else for whatever goes wrong!

MADAM: Shut up, what would you know?

ASHRAF: Keep a closer eye on Aiesha. (*Suddenly remembers.*) Oh ya-allah!! (*Goes to the door and shouts over to a member of staff.*) The beer barrels need changing!

MADAM: What do you mean about Aieshee?

ASHRAF: I've seen the way she's been behaving around the men and she's been acting that she's giving her heart to them.

MADAM: What and not just her body?

ASHRAF: Well…they keep feeling sorry for her and I don't know what she's been telling them.

MADAM: Look Ashraf you may be smitten with Pepsi and let him screw other guys, just remember we're not all like you, the girl has a heart.

ASHRAF: Oh since when have you been concerned about her heart?

MADAM: Since I've been seeing how you look at her.

ASHRAF: What do you mean?

MADAM: You used to do that to me. Make me feel I was nothing!

ASHRAF: Oh meri jaan. I was always true to you.

MADAM: Were you ever true to yourself?

ASHRAF: What is it, can't you be satisfied?

MADAM: Satisfied… Ashraf look at you trying to get Pepsi to have boobs put on.

ASHRAF: He wants them.

MADAM: Only because he thinks it'll please you.

ASHRAF: Well he's a kind boy.

MADAM: He's a boy who has nothing but you.

ASHRAF: For God's sake! Do you ever stop nagging?

MADAM: (*Calm.*) Listen, the new entertainment visa application forms have come, Aiesha's entertainment visa…let's renew it?

ASHRAF: Renew it! Are you crazy? She's a liability!

MADAM: Oh shut up. (*Pause.*) I've missed her. (*Pause.*) I feel close to her. She grew up with me. (*Pause.*) She's like my own.

ASHRAF: She'll stab you in the back.

MADAM: It's been two years since I last spent time with her, held her, lived with her, I've really missed her. She's only had a six-month visa.

ASHRAF: The punters will get bored, they need new girls!

MADAM: Just another three months?

ASHRAF: Stop spoiling my mood.

MADAM: Well think about it. (*Pause. She goes back to counting the money.*) That's….£735 from the dances.

ASHRAF: Make sure she behaves. I can't be dealing with any charity cases and those bloody women's refuge bitches coming round and having a good sniff like they did with the last little whore we had here.

MADAM: She's the best dancer we've had and brings in more money than any of the other girls ever did.

ASHRAF: There's plenty more where she came from.

MADAM: She goes then I go too.

ASHRAF: Where are you going to go?

MADAM: Back to Pakistan with her.

ASHRAF: Now I know you're really mad.

MADAM: Ashraf I've got enough money for Aiesha and me to rent a small room and live together and I can sew suits for girls to make some money.

ASHRAF: You've really worked this out.

MADAM: Aiesha deserves the best and I deserve more!

ASHRAF: I'm the man here…you can't demand anything from me.

MADAM: If you were a real man then I would have retired a long time ago, you'd be my pension.

ASHRAF: What is it with you…you always have to kill my mood?

He throws down his magazine in a tantrum and storms off.

MADAM: (*She starts to use the phone.*) Hello, salaam o
leikum bhai…it's Madam speaking…yes, yes never mind
all that git-mit [*chit-chat*] …I can see the weather is very
nice not quite Lahore weather.
Ahem…mmmm…yes…aha…have you any more
excuses? It's nearly 9 o'clock, you still haven't delivered
the paan mixes…is that why you go to masjid to talk
about us. We read namaz at home…not for show at the
masjid… Are we not good customers….we pay on
time…? Well?… Listen to me boy, I don't care and I'm
not scared of what the Masjid says, I haven't got time for
all this muska [*creeping*] if you're not here by 9.30 then
we'll not be shopping with you again…okay thank you
and khuda hafiz [*good bye*].

3lbs Rump Steak 4lbs Garnish

*Set on an empty stage just a mirror and PEPSI's memories. PEPSI
is about to start setting up the club and then starts looking in the
mirror admiring himself in a very feminine manner. He stops to
think. PEPSI begins talking to himself in the mirror. Impersonating
his father, a very butch and masculine character. PEPSI is in drag.*

PEPSI: So you think you're a man now do you? Well…?
All lanky and a few bits of bum-fluff poking out of your
chin…look at me you bastard. Look at me when I'm
talking to you…yes you…you weed. You're 15 and a
man. (*Violently slaps himself.*) Bitch keep out of this or do
you like it when your son peeps and spies on you…when
you're changing? Do you bitch? So boy, tell me? Why
you wearing your mum's sari? Tell me? You're dirty
little fucker…ma chaud [*mother fucker*].

*He stares at the mirror furious and frothing at the mouth.
This goes on for a minute or two.*

*AIESHA bursts in gigging, with a bottle of whiskey and a
glass. She notices PEPSI is reminiscing but doesn't let PEPSI
know. She knocks back a half glass of whiskey.*

PEPSI instantly jumps back into his own character.

AIESHA: Yes you look beautiful. Vain bitch. Come on
 Pepsi let's go darling.

*PEPSI fakes a giggle and AIESHA grabs him and they rush
off stage.*

4lbs Lamb Chops

*In the club. The evening performances are to begin. Disco lights are
softly flashing. Lollywood (Noor Jehan) music is playing in the
background. MADAM's eyes are wandering around, greeting the select
few customers that have booked in for the evening. She pours a cup of
tea from her flask and drinks it. Amongst them is a very nervous
CHARLES who comes and sits next to MADAM. The lighting and
sounds will give the effect that there are more people around; use the
audience if needed. MADAM has a tray with various paan mixe,
which she is wrapping and offering to the customers. She offers one to
CHARLES and he refuses. There are drinks and a large hookah
[tobacco bong]. Everyone has a puff now and then. The décor of the
club is of very Persian/Pakistani influence with rugs, big bolster
cushions and glittery curtains etc. The atmosphere is smoky and jolly.
The music changes to a song by UMI-10, 'Kaliyon ka chamon' ['The
sparkle of petals']. Applause and heckling. PEPSI and AIESHA
appear wearing dancing bells on their ankles. They kiss their hands,
touch the ground in front of their feet and then place each hand on
each ear. This is a way of asking for forgiveness before they dance. It
is a ritual before every dance. They begin miming to the song and
start to do an identical dance sequence that is provocative and seductive.*

CHARLES: My God what beauties.

MADAM: Aren't they just?

ASHRAF: (*Passes the paan.*) We're very blessed to see such
 jewels Charles.

CHARLES: No thanks.

ASHRAF: Go on Charles, it's all part of the service.

CHARLES: Okay. Thank you. (*Places the paan in his mouth and isn't too keen on the flavour.*)

They continue to watch the dance.

ASHRAF throws money at PEPSI to show his appreciation; PEPSI picks it up and shoves it in his bra.

CHARLES observes.

MADAM is always scanning around looking at other customers and playing coy but she does have her eye on one particular man.

The first dance finishes. Applause and heckling.

PEPSI is sitting talking and flirting with a customer.

AIESHA is also doing the same with another customer and so is MADAM. This uses the audience, which is given wads of fake £5 notes. These are to be thrown towards AIESHA and PEPSI as if from appreciative customers.

CHARLES and ASHRAF are watching.

CHARLES: That was amazing.

ASHRAF: Yes it was. They're good aren't they?

CHARLES: Good. They're bloody marvellous.

ASHRAF: Oh thank you.

CHARLES: I've never seen such a spectacle.

ASHRAF: Spectacle?

CHARLES: Well…it's so tasteful and respectful.

ASHRAF: You like tasteful and respectful?

CHARLES: Don't we all?

ASHRAF: Are you telling me that nothing happened in your trousers?

CHARLES: My God! Are you trying to embarrass me?

ASHRAF: No, no Charles. Of course I'm not. Just as one man to another?

CHARLES: I… I…

ASHRAF: I'll take that as a yes.

CHARLES: Honestly you're unbelievable!

ASHRAF: Tell me Charles which one do you like? Her? Or her?

CHARLES: They're both really beautiful.

ASHRAF: Ah yes they are, but which one would you save first from jumping off a cliff?

CHARLES: You do like to put people on the spot.

ASHRAF: Well man. Come on. Who's to go first off the cliff?

CHARLES: I'd say I'd save her first.

ASHRAF: Young man you have good taste.

CHARLES: Thanks.

ASHRAF: That is our lovely Aiesha.

CHARLES: She is beautiful.

ASHRAF: Go on, go and talk to her.

CHARLES: No, no I couldn't.

ASHRAF: What do you mean you couldn't?

CHARLES: She's busy talking to someone.

ASHRAF: Would you like to talk to her?

CHARLES: Yes I would but…

ASHRAF: There's no but about it. I'm going off to the little boy's room, so take your chance.

CHARLES: I couldn't.

ASHRAF: For goodness' sake boy. Here's your chance to learn a thing or two about women.

CHARLES: I'm hopeless with women.

ASHRAF: She's the best in the entertainment industry and she doesn't come cheap.

CHARLES knocks back his drink.

ASHRAF goes to AIESHA and whispers in her ear. She turns to CHARLES and smiles. She then continues with her conversation.

CHARLES pours himself another drink and sits nervously checking text messages on his phone.

AIESHA approaches and sits with him.

AIESHA: Are you not entertained enough?

CHARLES: Sorry?

AIESHA: Are you not entertained enough?

CHARLES: Yes I am. It was a fantastic dance.

AIESHA: It's just, you're very busy playing with your phone?

CHARLES: (*He fumbles and puts it away.*) No…no…it was just….

AIESHA: It was just you thought I hadn't noticed you?

CHARLES: No…no…not at all.

AIESHA: Well I did.

CHARLES: Really?

AIESHA: Yes you have kind eyes.

CHARLES: Thank you.

AIESHA: It's your first time here is it?

CHARLES: Um yes. I was just in the shop earlier and Ashraf invited me here.

AIESHA: Okay.

CHARLES: You dance beautifully.

AIESHA: Thank you.

CHARLES: Well actually it was amazing.

AIESHA: You like Pakistani dance?

CHARLES: To be honest I haven't really seen that much. Only occasionally on late night TV and I have a copy of *Dharma Veer* and *Kabi Kabi*.

AIESHA: I see. Bollywood not Lollywood. What's your name?

CHARLES: Charles. What's yours?

AIESHA: Aiesha.

CHARLES: That's pretty...pretty name for a pretty girl.

AIESHA: Thank you.

CHARLES: Have you been dancing for long?

AIESHA: Yes, since I was thirteen.

CHARLES: Oh really, what an art.

AIESHA: It's less of an art, more necessity.

PEPSI approaches.

PEPSI: Next dance is due to start.

CHARLES: Excellent stuff. I'm looking forward to it already.

PEPSI: It'll be a mesmerising number.

CHARLES: So, maybe we can speak later?

PEPSI: You'll have to talk to Madam about that.

AIESHA: Yes maybe.

> *Music starts to play and PEPSI and AIESHA start the next dance. The song by Noor Jehan, 'Gulla guria karah dee teray nal veh. Kisay de null gull nah kareeh'* ['We'll have deep chats but don't tell anyone about them']. *Applause, heckling and small showers of £5 notes.*

> *AIESHA just dances to tempt and tease CHARLES. MADAM gestures at her not to neglect the other customers, who are happily throwing money her way. AIESHA only makes half-hearted attempts to please the others. Her heart is set on CHARLES.*

> *The audience is throwing money at PEPSI and AIESHA and so CHARLES joins in by throwing cash into the dance area.*

> *During their dance, PEPSI and AIESHA collect the money and stuff it into their cleavage or waistbands. AIESHA and PEPSI go to the black bag next to MADAM and put the money in the bag, the symbol of her power. The dance ends.*

> *MADAM sits with CHARLES, and AIESHA sits alone fixing her ankle bells. She keeps looking over at CHARLES and he returns the looks.*

> *PEPSI and ASHRAF are having a little canoodle.*

MADAM: You like my little Aiesha?

CHARLES: I didn't know she was your daughter…sorry.

MADAM: Don't be sorry. She is here to be appreciated. I've raised her, trained her but she's not mine.

CHARLES: Well you've done a superb job.

MADAM: Thank you. I was once like her.

CHARLES: Tell me. Does Ashraf not mind you talking to other men. You know, you two being married.

MADAM: Goodness. Married? To him? Never! He's as bent as a rusty rupee coin.

CHARLES: Bent? What do you mean?

MADAM: Are you really stupid or pretending to be. I'm sorry. (*Pause.*) I was in love with him once. But now he likes his own kind. He's, you know, gay.

CHARLES: But he's all over that beautiful girl?

MADAM: Charles. That girl is a boy.

CHARLES: Ah right…right. I must seem a right idiot.

MADAM: Yes. But it's not your fault. You seem a successful idiot…man, I mean.

CHARLES: … I'm lost for words.

MADAM: Don't be lost. Just come to us. (*Laughs.*) As a rule I don't normally let people in for free. You have to be a member and pay at the door.

CHARLES: Oh I'm sorry.

MADAM: No, no. Tonight you are my guest but next time…will there be a next time?

CHARLES: Oh Madam. I feel totally spoilt. Yes I'd love there to be a next time.

MADAM: On the way out, get yourself registered and they'll tell you all about the pricing system.

CHARLES: Oh right. Is it time to leave?

MADAM: No, no. You stay and enjoy yourself. (*She notices him looking at AIESHA.*) But my Aiesha doesn't come free with tonight's delights. You'll have to pay extra.

CHARLES: Pay?

MADAM: Sorry.

CHARLES: No, no don't be…it's just… I didn't realise.

MADAM: It does seem a bit harsh but she is in demand. If you can pay more than that gentleman has offered then I can arrange for Aiesha to spend the rest of the evening with you and you can fulfil your heart's desires. But, if you think she's not worth it, then that's a different matter.

CHARLES: Heart's desires?… (*He thinks for a few seconds.*) How much?

MADAM: She's not cheap Charles.

CHARLES: How much?

MADAM: Look, think about it. I don't want you feeling pressured. Mr Tarsem has already proposed an offer of £200 for the night plus whatever else he might like to give our Aiesha. (*Pause.*)

CHARLES: How does £300 sound to you?

MADAM: Well it sounds good but if there's someone who offers more then we'll have to renegotiate.

Musical overlap.

MADAM pours herself a cup of tea from her flask and drinks it. Money is exchanged discreetly. She then goes over to AIESHA who is talking to another customer and whispers in her ear. Scene ends with AIESHA sitting with CHARLES.

5lbs Turkey Breast

Set in the bedrooms of Bells. Some days have passed since CHARLES had his first visit to Bells. There are three different glittery see-through curtains (gold, parrot green, cerise red) at the front of the stage, with strong lighting behind them. Thus the audience can see silhouettes of the cast. Behind each curtain there are couples having sex at Bells. On the left-hand side is ASHRAF and PEPSI with ASHRAF buggering PEPSI. In the middle is AIESHA and CHARLES with AIESHA on top of CHARLES. They are all naked. On the right hand side is MADAM wearing her shalvar kameez and dupatta on her head, with a naked CUSTOMER on a lead on all fours. She's playing a dominatrix. The background music is a classical tune by Nusrat Fateh Ali Khan, similar to a Sufi chant.

ASHRAF: (*Moans and groans.*) Yes! Yes! You dirty bitch. I saw you flirting with those men out there.

PEPSI: (*Moans and groans.*) Oh! Oh! But you know I love you?

ASHRAF: Yes! Yes! Did you want their cock or mine?

PEPSI: Ah! Ah! Yours baby yours baby.

ASHRAF: Ah! Ah! Am I good to you?

PEPSI: The best, the best!

MADAM: Bite me?

CUSTOMER 1: Rraaaaaaaahhhhh!!!

MADAM: Not like that. (*Slap.*)

CUSTOMER 1: Ow, ow, ow!!!

MADAM: Gently.

CUSTOMER 1: Slurp, slurp...

MADAM: That's it.

CUSTOMER 1: Aahhh rrrrrrrrr!!!

MADAM: Lick me here…and now here?

CUSTOMER 1: Woof woof…

MADAM: Lick my feet.

CUSTOMER 1: Ow ow ow!!!

CHARLES and AIESHA are in the afterglow of having had sex.

AIESHA is sitting on CHARLES, she is gently stroking his face. He stops her and sits up.

CHARLES: Sweetheart… How many days have I been coming to visit you, two, three? I've lost count. I feel… I…

AIESHA: Look, lie down, it's fine.

CHARLES: But I want you to know I…

AIESHA: (*She kisses him.*) That you…. what?

CHARLES: That I really like you… I know we've only just met…but I feel there's something more there.

AIESHA: Of course there is.

CHARLES: Yes…please tell me there is? So that I know that I'm not imagining it.

AIESHA: Oh Charles there's so many like you that fall in love every night and then go back to their own little worlds.

CHARLES: No I'm not like that. I don't want to know about the others. I'm talking about you and me.

AIESHA: Nobody has a 'you and me' with a whore.

CHARLES: Don't say that. You're different. You're precious.

AIESHA: Okay Charles. (*She gets off.*)

CHARLES: What?

AIESHA: You want me to play your girl?

CHARLES: No, no. Look, I'll promise to come back every weekend and you can phone me or I'll phone you.

AIESHA: Charles stop this. You don't know me. You know nothing!

CHARLES: I know how I feel. (*She cries and he hugs her.*)

AIESHA: You don't. How could you? Do I come from a good family, do I miss them? What do I feel?

CHARLES: 'I remember I never could catch you,
For no one could match you,
You had wonderful, luminous, fleet
Little wings to your feet.'

AIESHA: Poetry…you like books?

CHARLES: Yes, I love to read.

AIESHA: I like poetry, I love books, they make me feel… safe, close to my family.

CHARLES: Really? I read to escape from everything and everyone.

AIESHA: Oh me too. I escape all the time.

CHARLES: Have you read Oscar Wilde?

AIESHA: No I haven't, but I remember my father reading.

CHARLES: Your father must have fine taste…where is your family?

AIESHA: (*She gets into daydream mode and ignores his question.*) Yes, I suppose he must have great taste.

CHARLES: Tell me, what's your favourite book?

AIESHA: No. You'll laugh.

CHARLES: Promise I won't.

AIESHA: *Tom's Midnight Garden*; it's the last book my father gave me. Tom and me had our adventures in my garden in Pakistan. Pretty with flowers and insects clicking away and the different perfumes…

CHARLES: Sounds beautiful, just like you. So you had books in English?

AIESHA: Of course silly.

CHARLES: I just thought you'd be reading everything in your language?

AIESHA: Language doesn't belong, it's not mine or yours, it's for sharing.

CHARLES: Share with me?

AIESHA: In Urdu, I love *Laila Majnu*. It's like *Romeo and Juliet*. I think I remember my father telling me that Laila was originally a black woman, beautiful and innocent. Their love was true but very innocent.

CHARLES: Ah, romance and true love.

AIESHA: I believe in true love.

CHARLES: Who's it by…Laila?

AIESHA: You won't be able to get it, it's an old classic and it's in Urdu.

CHARLES: There must be translations?

AIESHA: Maybe, probably.

CHARLES: Anyway if not, you can read it to me in Urdu?

AIESHA: But you won't understand.

CHARLES: It'll be lovely just to hear the words come out of your mouth.

AIESHA: Silly.

AIESHA sings the Hindi song 'Barbaad-e-mohabbat Ki Dua Hindi' from the Movie/Album Laila Majnu. *(Hindi Lyrics.)*

'Barabaad e mohabbat ki duaa saath lie jaa
[*Take with you the ruined prayers of my love*]
tootaa huaa ikaraar-e-vafaa saath lie jaa
[*take with you the broken consent of my commitment*]
tapati hui raahon mein tujhe aanch na pahunche
diivaane ki ashkon ki ghataa saath lie jaa
barabaad e mohabbat ki duaa saath lie jaa.'

CHARLES: Wow, you amaze me.

AIESHA: (*Giggling.*) No…no… You say vah vah, adaab.

She gestures with her hand the correct way to acknowledge an artist: right hand poised and then raised in front of the nose and head slightly bowed.

CHARLES: Vah vah, adaab. (*He imitates her gestures.*)

CHARLES: I always had such boring books to read.

They chuckle. She kisses his body but not his lips and caresses him. To the audience it's clear she's doing her job and manipulating.

CHARLES: (*Moans and groans.*) Oh! Oh! You're so beautiful.

AIESHA: Am I really?

CHARLES: You're my Cleopatra.

AIESHA: Wasn't she sometimes bad to her men?

CHARLES: You could never be bad.

AIESHA: Do you like it when I do this?

CHARLES: Ouch…oh yes.

AIESHA: And this…

She goes down on him with her back to the audience using her dupatta [scarf] to flirtatiously cover her head. We hear moans and groans from both of them.

CHARLES: Oh…o…o…oo! Mmm… What have I done to deserve you?

He reaches orgasm prematurely and uses the dupatta to wipe himself clean. He lovingly caresses her at the same time.

AIESHA: Paid a price…

He hugs her and then attempts to kiss her. She subtly moves her face so that his kiss lands on her cheek, and doesn't reciprocate his hugs with such intensity.

They sleep.

Eventually CHARLES gets dressed. He looks at AIESHA sleeping. Noticing the time on his watch he tiptoes out.

6lbs Chicken Drumsticks

A bedroom at Bells. A few days later AIESHA and PEPSI are relaxing in their bedroom. PEPSI is painting his nails and AIESHA is reading a book.

PEPSI: Aiesha baby, why have you always got your head stuck in books?

AIESHA: I haven't!

PEPSI: Yes you have!

AIESHA: Well it's not as often as I'd like. This is such a wonderful book. I love it, Charles gave it to me.

PEPSI: Six nights in a row?

AIESHA: He pays, doesn't he?

PEPSI: Well don't bother getting too hooked on that book. You know what happens to all your books, they get binned, baby!

AIESHA: I know. I hate it. It's so painful to see them thrown away. All those lovely words that describe life and let you into people's minds.

PEPSI: You're weird.

AIESHA: Charles likes to read.

PEPSI: Yeah right.

AIESHA: He does. He told me a poem that I'll always keep in my memory.

PEPSI: You best keep it in your memory. Don't start getting funny ideas about writing notes to people and leaving them around to be found.

AIESHA: I won't!

PEPSI: Cos you know Madam and Ashraf won't just stop at throwing every book you read, they'll stop you reading. Full-stop-comma-comma-dash-dash! If you hadn't left 'HELP' notes in the books, for the librarians to find you'd…

AIESHA: I know. I know. I don't need a lecture from you.

PEPSI: Well girlfriend that's why your books get binned.

AIESHA: Okay will you be quiet…go look at yourself in the mirror or something.

PEPSI: (*Sticks his tongue out at her in disgust.*) Anyway what was this poem he read?

AIESHA: It was lovely.

PEPSI: Was it dirty…like horny stuff?

AIESHA: No silly. It was real. Really….

PEPSI: Oh no, here we go, another girl lusting for a loser. You only just got off the boat a few months ago darling. Calm down. Just because he's an educated desi, it doesn't make him all that different. Stuck up git…

AIESHA: I'm not lusting and he's not a loser.

PEPSI: Well what is he?

AIESHA: He's kind and you can…

PEPSI: And what! You'll live happily ever after? Darling listen to me. Your visa is only for six months and you're halfway through it already.

AIESHA: Madam will extend it.

PEPSI: Not if she finds out what you're doing.

AIESHA: I'm not doing anything.

PEPSI: Playing games with the customers is doing something. Your arse is money to feed us and keep you living in style. (*Warning her.*) Okay? No 'in love' games!

AIESHA: We play love games all the time. What's so wrong?

PEPSI: You're serious about conning this one. That's what's wrong.

AIESHA: No, I'm not doing anything. You've got Ashraf.

PEPSI: And you've got a ticket back to Pakistan waiting for you.

AIESHA: I can't go back there. Not now.

PEPSI: Why not?

AIESHA: Pepsi you chose not to see your family. I never had a choice. I got raped and kidnapped by my father's enemies. Over what, a bit of land in Pakistan? Am I to suffer forever? I suppose you think I'm making it up but it's true, that's what happens. Pepsi?

PEPSI: Look don't do this to me! Why do you girls put me through this shit? Every one of you has your own fucking sob story.

AIESHA: It's true. You don't know what it's like. I was dropped off at Madam's in the middle of the night wearing just a dirty shawl covered in my blood. I have nothing. Nothing of my own. They said they were going to take my torn clothes back to my father as a trophy. My father's old, it must have killed him. I was thirteen Pepsi. Thirteen!

PEPSI: Look shit happens. I'm sorry.

AIESHA: Fine. Who was I trying to fool? Thinking you might have a heart. Don't you ever get tired of laughing in the face of the world?

PEPSI: Look don't put that emotional guilt shit on me. I get enough of that from everyone else. Ashraf will kill me if he finds out that we're even talking about these things.

AIESHA: I won't tell him. Pleeaase?

PEPSI: For fuck's sake…What do you want me to do?

AIESHA: I want you to help me catch him, think what fun we'll have winding Charles up and then I'll do the rest.

PEPSI: How the hell am I supposed to do that?

AIESHA: Just tell him that I think about him all the time and I talk about him and can't sleep…

PEPSI: Yeah right.

AIESHA: Use your brain Pepsi. And I'll write him poems and you can give them to him.

PEPSI: No, no fucking way, I'm not playing posty.

AIESHA: Okay, okay forget the poems.

PEPSI: What you gonna do once he's convinced about you?

AIESHA: I told you, leave it to me.

PEPSI: Girlfriend I hope you know what you're doing.

AIESHA: I think I do.

PEPSI: You know, there's no such thing as freedom?

AIESHA: You tell me if there's not freedom after hearing words like:
'I remember I never could catch you,
For no one could match you,
You had wonderful, luminous, fleet
Little wings to your feet.'

PEPSI: Little wings to your feet? You'll have a bloody ball and chain if you get caught.

6½ lbs Calf Heart

Set in the bedrooms of Bells. Outside there are sounds of cat fights and rubbish cans kicked by a passer by. Lights are just on ASHRAF, MADAM and AIESHA.

A melodic Islamic call for prayer plays on the broken decorative Azan clock.

Lights vary from ASHRAF (who is in the butcher's shop), MADAM and AIESHA.

ASHRAF, MADAM and AIESHA are all occupied reading Namaz. They're at various stages of either having read Namaz or folding up their prayer mats, to being completely absorbed in prayer. But everyone is silent as prayer times are the rare moments of tranquillity at Bells. There is some slight interaction between characters when they're not reading Namaz but this is just merely to pass a book to each other or to shove up on the sofa.

Both AIESHA and MADAM have their heads covered with their dupatta and ASHRAF is wearing a prayer hat. PEPSI is lying down with his headphones on listening to his music and reading a magazine. The three finish Namaz and fold up their mats.

7lbs Tripe

Garnish. Set on an empty or blacked out stage. Just a mirror and PEPSI's memories. PEPSI is looking in the mirror, admiring himself in a very feminine manner. He stops to think. He begins talking to himself in the mirror. Impersonating his mother, a very nervous character.

PEPSI: Ranjeet please be good, try not to get your father angry? Wear your pugg [*turban*]? You know it'll please him. Why do you keep behaving like this? We're Sikh, we are proud and would die for our people. You can't wear a bit of fabric on your head for your father's sake? What about for my sake? Do you like it when I get beaten for your mistakes? Do you? Ranjeet. Tell me? What have I done to deserve a son like you? Tell me Guru Ji. Why me? Instead of wrapping six yards of sari around your waist just wrap it on your head? If you can't do that much for me then I have no son. I never gave birth to you. You're a miscarriage, a miscarriage of my life, my fortune, my happiness and my health. A miscarriage…

PEPSI sits there holding himself. ASHRAF walks in smiling holding his Breasts'r'Us *magazine. He's seen PEPSI sitting there, trembling. ASHRAF holds PEPSI lovingly and comforts him.*

Lights fade.

8lbs Liver

Set in the club. Scene opens with AIESHA dancing to a Hadiqa song 'Boohey Barian' ['Doors, windows, I wanna jump these walls']. *She spends most of the performance avoiding CHARLES. CHARLES is trying to draw her attention to him by throwing money at her but she only acknowledges him for momentary encounters as she takes his money. Other customers are getting a lot more attention from AIESHA. MADAM is with her flask of tea and is entertaining her men, also keeping her eye on what's going on. PEPSI is busy serving drinks and chatting with customers. CHARLES is a bit drunk by the end of AIESHA's dance. Applause and heckling from the audience. AIESHA sits and chats with another customer. PEPSI joins CHARLES.*

PEPSI: Wasn't she just fab?

CHARLES: Yes she was.

PEPSI: Don't you just love the way she has her final spin and her skirt rises so high that you can see her undies?

CHARLES: Super spin. She is just fab.

PEPSI: I always wear knickers that contrast with my outfits; I think it's much more spectacular. But Aieshee always likes hers to match.

CHARLES: Aieshee, Aieshee… I like matching undies… Tell me Pepsi I've been coming here for the last two weeks, nearly every night. I…

PEPSI: You sure have.

CHARLES: I somehow feel that the last few days she's been a bit distant from me. Have I done something to upset her?

PEPSI: No silly, you must be imagining it.

CHARLES: No really. I'm not.

PEPSI: What makes you think that?

CHARLES: Just that she spends more time with those guys than me.

PEPSI: Well darling this is a business and you don't have the monopoly. Even as a clever accountant. The money doesn't roll in by itself.

CHARLES: Yes, yes I understand that but?

PEPSI: But what? You want her to sit with you all night, sucking just your dick?

CHARLES: What? Don't be disgusting!

PEPSI: Look Charles I don't mean to be rude but you have her every night as long as you offer the most money to Madam. One night when you're not here, Aieshee will still have to have someone else zooming her.

CHARLES: Why are you talking so foul?

PEPSI: I'm not talking foul.

CHARLES: I'm not stupid. I do know how these things work. I want her to be happy with me. I want to make her happy.

PEPSI: I'm telling you how it is. You men just need a hole but us women...well we're a bit more particular about what goes in and when we don't have a choice...we learn to switch off our emotions.

CHARLES: What you saying? She has no emotions for me?

PEPSI: No that's not what I said. (*Flirts.*) Stop getting your pants all screwed up... I might start thinking you want me.

CHARLES: Well what do you mean?

PEPSI: She has loads of emotions for you Charles.

CHARLES: Really?

PEPSI: She never stops talking about you.

CHARLES: No, you're kidding me?

PEPSI: No, I'm not kidding.

CHARLES: God. I can be such an idiot. Tell me, what does she say?

PEPSI: Look, I can't just go round telling you my friend's secrets…

CHARLES pulls out some money. PEPSI places it in his bra.

I really mustn't. She'll kill me. She thinks I will take everything to the grave with me.

CHARLES impatiently offers him more money.

Coorrr! You pouring more money at me like this, I might have to bend over for you tonight instead of my Ashraf. (*Slightly worried.*) Don't make it obvious for God's sake.

Applause and heckling.

AIESHA starts to dance in the background.

The music is loud. She avoids eye contact with CHARLES but dances provocatively around him, teasing him by making him feel her presence whilst her attention is on other men.

CHARLES: Sorry, sorry, you don't know what it's like to have met someone special.

PEPSI: You sure you don't want me instead, I'm cheaper and just as good?

CHARLES: Pepsi please tell me. You're beautiful but Aiesha is my special girl. What does Aiesha think of me? I spend almost every night with her, I should know her. But because I pay she has to be polite.

PEPSI: No sir, you're wrong. Not our Aieshee, she doesn't have to be nice to anyone. You see…people want her, she's the top prize and so the men are grateful that they get her at the end of the night. Madam lets her choose which one. So why do you think you're the lucky guy who gets her at the end of the night?

CHARLES: Not because I've paid the highest?

PEPSI: Well yes because you've paid the highest but Aieshee is Madam's favourite, so it's always Aieshee's opinion that counts. And so my handsome Charles she chooses you every time.

CHARLES: Really. I can't believe it. Me?

PEPSI: Yes and if that doesn't tell you how she feels then I don't know what will.

CHARLES: Tell me Pepsi, what I can do to impress her that little bit more…you know shall I buy her a gift…shall I get her flowers….or what?

PEPSI: Look Charles…how do I say this without frightening you away?

CHARLES: Tell me. You won't frighten me. I need to know.

PEPSI: Well, I shouldn't but…

CHARLES: Pepsiiiiii please get on with it!

PEPSI: Okay. Charles you promise never to tell?

CHARLES: I promise.

PEPSI: You don't need to be buying her gifts. She doesn't stop thinking about you. She's memorised your poem.

CHARLES: My poem?

PEPSI: Yeah, that one about the wings on her feet or something?

CHARLES: My magic, exotic, mystical Oscar Wilde.

PEPSI: Fuck knows, tell her another poem 'cos that one's pissing me off. It'd piss you off too, hearing it fifteen times a day.

CHARLES: She likes my Oscar Wilde?

PEPSI: You sound surprised. Is it a regular chat-up line, to read poems to your girls?

CHARLES: No, no, not at all. Wilde was a great man, he idolised beauty for beauty's sake…the mystical East. I just thought it very appropriate. If I knew an Urdu poem I would've recited that.

PEPSI: Good. I was gonna to say…you'd scare them off. It's only book-worms like Aieshee that are into all that poetry rubbish. False hopes and bad rhyming!

CHARLES: Good rhyming, I'll have you know. What else does she say about me then?

PEPSI: Cough up mate, it's expensive being a woman.

CHARLES: Sorry…here.

PEPSI: That's a bit better. She says you're a caring gentle fuck. That you listen to her and even though you're pretending, she feels you really care.

CHARLES: I do care, I do.

PEPSI: Darling everyone pretends with a whore.

CHARLES: Don't call her that.

PEPSI: Oh, don't get all high and mighty.

CHARLES: Sorry…but she's special, she's a Pakistani jewel.

PEPSI: Look we're all special but our specialities always stay within these four walls. Beyond that we have no more value than my Ashraf's leftover tripe.

CHARLES: (*Assertively.*) As a regular paying member… (*Softens.*) We're not all weird you know. I'm also an Indian. I do understand some things.

Applause and heckling.

AIESHA finishes her dance and sits with a customer who is obviously treating her a bit rough. She gets up and moves to another customer. Both CHARLES and PEPSI notice this.

AIESHA: Besharam…tere ghar mah, bhein nahee? [*Shameless…have you no mother or sister at home?*]

PEPSI: Well that's a matter of opinion.

CHARLES: Somebody must have really hurt you Pepsi.

PEPSI: Somebody needs to stick a red-hot poker up your arse to wake you up and smell the shit!

CHARLES: I'm awake. I've never been so awake ever before. Aiesha brings all my senses to life.

PEPSI: Obviously not your common sense.

CHARLES: You're so cynical.

PEPSI: What's cynical? 'Cos if it's like clinical then I might have to slap you.

CHARLES: No, no, cynical is like a sceptic, an unbeliever, a Pepsi who doesn't trust.

PEPSI: I trust you'll buy me whatever you were intending to buy for Aiesha. She's happy with poxy poetry. Me, I'm a material girl.

She sings Madonna's version of 'Material Girl'.

CHARLES joins in as well. Giggling.

MADAM: Pepsi darling, are you going to sit there all night boring poor Charles?

CHARLES: She's fine Madam.

PEPSI: Oh well I'm off. I fancy a little boogie anyway.

MADAM sits with CHARLES.

PEPSI starts to dance in classical Pakistani combined with western styles to Madonna's 'Justify my love'. There's big applause and heckling.

PEPSI starts off on his own but halfway through AIESHA joins him and they both synchronise their dance.

They seem to be having a good time.

MADAM: My god. Pepsi loves this Madonna. She seems to me to be the Noor Jehan of your world.

ASHRAF rushes in wiping his face clean. He's been spat at and his clothes are bedraggled.

What happened to you?

CHARLES: Bloody hell, are you all right?

ASHRAF: Yes, yes I'm fine.

CHARLES: What happened?

ASHRAF: It's a couple of the bastards from the Masjid.

CHARLES: Masjid?

ASHRAF: The mosque… Sufi Gulab!

MADAM: Sufi Galub, the little… (*Tells CHARLES.*) Protesting that we are not Islami?

ASHRAF: Kaffir, devil worshippers…fucking flower seller.

MADAM: And the bloody police are useless.

CHARLES: But surely the mosque…well they're out of order for being violent.

ASHRAF: Yes they are but who's going to stop them?

CHARLES: It's terrible!

MADAM: Let's just keep it down. It'll upset the customers. Anyway it's not everyone at the Masjid, it's just the little haramis [*bastards*] like Sufi Gulab.

CHARLES: Who is this Sufi Gulab? Look, is there anything I can do to help?

ASHRAF: No thank you Charles. Unless you want to work as a doorman because I've just lost one guy. He's resigned.

CHARLES: Sorry, I think I'd be useless doing that.

AIESHA notices ASHRAF and rushes over.

PEPSI is lost in the music.

AIESHA: What happened to you?

MADAM: Nothing, nothing, you get on with your work.

AIESHA tries to give ASHRAF a supportive stroke but he pushes her off aggressively. She cowers up to CHARLES who tries to comfort her. They sit hugging.

ASHRAF: Didn't you hear Madam?

MADAM: Get on with your work.

ASHRAF: Act like there's nothing wrong.

CHARLES: Why is the mosque objecting? I thought this sort of thing went on openly in our culture?

AIESHA: Nothing goes on openly in our culture, don't you even know that? (*She leaves.*)

ASHRAF: What do you mean Charles, openly?

CHARLES: Well I just thought…

MADAM: You just thought we like our women as whores?

ASHRAF: Thoughts like that Charles it's better not to think!

CHARLES: No, no, that's not what I meant. I was actually thinking about it in historical terms where it was socially acceptable to initiate your son into puberty by taking him to a cou.

ASHRAF: That's a fucking dream world…

CHARLES: The Moguls?

ASHRAF: There was a mosque meeting today and they were discussing Bells.

MADAM: What about Bells?

ASHRAF : That we're a whorehouse…koota [*dog*] Sufi Gulab.

MADAM: Is that what they said?

ASHRAF: God knows.

MADAM: There are English clubs like this… Minty Rhino's, so why don't they get called whorehouses?

ASHRAF: Because it's our people. They want to look honourable and have a cheap wank.

MADAM: Next time, when that boy from the Masjid delivers the paan mix, you see what I do to him.

ASHRAF: Cheap bastard.

MADAM: Always wants to sit for a quick drink.

ASHRAF: I bet he doesn't tell them that at the mosque.

MADAM: Double standards!

ASHRAF: Look at the Halaal meat delivery boy.

MADAM: Always delivers last to us and then begs to stay.

CHARLES: I know a few of the local councillors for the Labour party.

MADAM: Good for you.

CHARLES: No listen, they're my drinking buddies. They're Pakistani like you.

ASHRAF: Well they'll be the biggest two-faced bastards.

CHARLES: Yes well, I helped them out with some sticky accounts or lack of accounts, from which they've saved a penny or two. I'm sure I can pull some favours.

ASHRAF: They won't listen to you.

CHARLES: Yes they will.

ASHRAF: You can't put yourself in that position.

CHARLES: We go back from my first paan and their first lager.

ASHRAF: And what, now it's their first brothel?

MADAM: And your first Masjid?

CHARLES: Well… It's worth a try?

ASHRAF: Yes, I suppose you're right.

CHARLES: And… I think, a colleague of mine, her husband's a chief superintendent.

ASHRAF: Mmmm…

MADAM: Oh well…yes…maybe.

CHARLES: Yes and he may be able to pull a few strings in the community.

ASHRAF: Really?

MADAM: That sounds better.

ASHRAF: I don't think you'll have much luck with the local councillors.

MADAM: They're the ones who sell their own daughters to get a vote.

CHARLES: Look, tomorrow morning first thing, I'll personally pop in to see the chief.

MADAM: Charles you're so kind.

CHARLES: Really it's nothing.

MADAM: Well thank you, but…

ASHRAF: Would you be able to talk to them about my planning application for a new building extension to the shop as well?

CHARLES: A new building extension?

MADAM: Shut up Ashraf, let's go and clean you up…stupid idiot…building extension…honestly I don't believe you sometimes.

MADAM and ASHRAF leave.

AIESHA returns.

AIESHA: So now you're a real hero?

CHARLES: I'll do anything to get into their good books. I want you to be mine.

AIESHA: Pay the price and I'm yours.

CHARLES: What about if I don't pay the price?

AIESHA: Well... Then maybe I might be yours or maybe not.

CHARLES: This is ridiculous, you can't live like this... (*Sympathetically.*) It must be frightening for you.

AIESHA: (*Child-like.*) Are you suggesting living together?

CHARLES: (*He pauses and thinks about it.*) Uuuumm ye... Yes!

AIESHA: I would never fit in to your world.

CHARLES: Our world. I could write to your father and explain that you are safe with me. I could send him money.

AIESHA: No, no, then they'll be suspicious of where he got the money.

CHARLES: Who's they? I can sort something out.

AIESHA: No you don't understand, they took me as a revenge for him not paying his debts. They'll think he had the money all along and just didn't want me...as his daughter. (*Pause.*) He'll be old now and my mum, she probably never leaves the prayer mat.

CHARLES: Aiesha, Aiesha, Aiesha, your parents love you more than you know and your mum's probably praying for a peaceful life for you. I love you. I never thought that this could happen to me. But it has. Please believe me.

AIESHA: Ssssh Charles let's not talk. We only say things we might regret.

CHARLES: You're always avoiding talking about these things. I want to know you. I want you to trust me.

AIESHA: Ssshhh, please…what would your Oscar say at a time like this?

CHARLES: (*Pauses as he tries to think of a poem.*)
'And her sweet red lips on these lips of mine
Burned like the ruby fire set
In the swinging lamp of a crimson shrine,
Or the bleeding wounds of the pomegranate,
Or the heart of the lotus drenched and wet
With the spilt-out blood of the rose-red wine.'

AIESHA: God! Oscar you're brilliant.

CHARLES: I want you to love me…know me…

9lbs Kidneys

A bedroom at Bells. Later that evening. ASHRAF is sitting reading his magazine, nursing his face and drinking a cup of tea. MADAM is lying with her head on his lap. She is humming songs and caressing her arms and bracelets in a fidgety, flirty manner. ASHRAF shows no interest other than an occasional smile just to please her. PEPSI flirtatiously walks in to get a make-up bag. ASHRAF's eyes light up. PEPSI leaves. ASHRAF instantly gets up without any concern for MADAM's comfort and follows PEPSI offstage. MADAM is hurt and annoyed.

ASHRAF: I'm very tired.

MADAM: (*Shouts out to ASHRAF.*) Send Aieshee in. Her hair needs doing. You bloody miserable dog.

PEPSI: (*Off.*) Last prick out!

ASHRAF: (*Off.*) Good, okay

PEPSI & ASHRAF: (*Off, giggling.*) Aieshee, Madam wants you.

MADAM switches on the cassette player. There is music in the background.

AIESHA walks in reading her book. Without looking around she automatically sits in front of MADAM.

MADAM oils, combs and plaits AIESHA's hair. MADAM's flask is next to her.

AIESHA is trying to read her book. AIESHA occasionally passes MADAM a hair-band to tie up her plaits. They are both wearing simple shalvar kameez suits.

MADAM: Look up will you?

AIESHA: I am.

MADAM: How am I supposed to brush your hair if you've got your head stuck in a book?

AIESHA: Ouch!

MADAM: I thought you'd finished all the books we got for you last week?

AIESHA: Yes, I have but I thought I'd read this one again.

MADAM: I don't know how you do it.

AIESHA: Do what?

MADAM: Read all these books.

AIESHA: Because they're interesting and I learn about the world.

MADAM: Oh my dear child learning about the world isn't in books.

AIESHA: Well where is it?

MADAM: It's everywhere you look.

AIESHA: I only get to look where I'm told and that's usually up someone's bottom.

MADAM: Well there you have it, that's the real world.

AIESHA: I see.

MADAM: (*Jokes.*) Ashraf could get you biology books.

AIESHA: Madam, do you love Ashraf ji?

MADAM: Do I love the old fool?

AIESHA: Yes, love him.

MADAM: Love is complicated.

AIESHA: What do you mean?

MADAM: Love can be painful and it can be dishonourable too.

AIESHA: Love is what we all want.

MADAM: Yes, but what we get is another thing.

AIESHA: I want love.

MADAM: I know you do my sweet.

AIESHA: I'm going to get it.

MADAM: You have it now.

AIESHA: No I don't.

MADAM: Aieshee, I love you.

AIESHA: For the money I make you.

MADAM: Is that what you think?

AIESHA: Well, Madam if you really loved me you would have let me go back to my parents when I first got dumped at your home in Heera Mandi.

MADAM: We've had this conversation time and time again. Your family would have killed you just to prove how honourable they were, how they weren't going to allow a soiled girl back into their house.

AIESHA: You keep telling me that but you never knew my father. He's understanding, he would be…

MADAM: …be okay that you were raped by men that he has to see everyday and can't do anything to?

AIESHA: No, that's not what I meant.

MADAM: He'd be okay seeing you go through the pain and humiliation of all the questions and insinuations made upon your honour?

AIESHA: He loved me, he would have…

MADAM: Yes he loved you and this way he still does…you're his little girl…his Parveen. Let him remember you as that.

AIESHA: Why didn't you have a baby?

MADAM: And risk having a daughter, bring a child into my little world? And who would be the father… Ashraf?

AIESHA: You said you used to have men falling at your feet.

MADAM: Darling, men always fall at your feet when they're drunk.

AIESHA: You never told me whether you love Ashraf Ji.

MADAM: Yes I love him, loved him and I wanted to be his. He didn't want me.

AIESHA: Why did you stay with him?

MADAM: He loves me, in his own little way. When he bought me from my Naika [*madam*] she was furious. Madam never wanted me to leave. You'd been with us for about four years when I left.

AIESHA: Really?

MADAM: I was old and not bringing in the money. You younger girls were fresh and profitable. Ashraf's offer to set up a mujra club in England and send money back to Lahore was what tempted my Naika.

AIESHA: I always thought that when you'd left you'd run away.

MADAM: No my little book-worm, there's no point me running away. And with who? Ashraf who loves me more like his pet dog?

AIESHA: It couldn't have always been like that.

MADAM: No at first we were lovers but then…then he was free to change his mind.

AIESHA: I want to be free.

MADAM: We all do. But freedom is in the heart and with those who love you. I was cheated out of my freedom.

AIESHA: Nobody loves me.

MADAM: Shut up silly. If nobody loved you, you'd not be here. I fought hard for Naika to let you come to England and for you to have your books. I fought…

AIESHA: They're not good books.

MADAM: What do you mean?

AIESHA: I want the books that I want to read, not the books that Ashraf ji chooses for me.

MADAM: Really, so what books do you want to read?

AIESHA: Like Oscar Wilde. Charles reads Oscar Wilde.

MADAM: I'll get you Oscar Wilde if you want, but you watch that Charles.

AIESHA: No, he's really okay, not like other customers. Just lost and looking for love.

MADAM: With the money he's got, he doesn't have to be lost.

AIESHA: Really Madam, he's the only one who plays with my mind and not just my body.

MADAM: Don't start dreaming up all sorts with men who can read a little more than our price list… What is it with you and reading?

AIESHA: (*Angry.*) Reading makes me feel I'm with my father that's what! (*She storms off.*) You say you love me but you can't give me my family, can you?

MADAM: We are your family and I do understand, you don't understand.

AIESHA: No you don't understand me. Charles does, his zindagi [*life*] is like mine.

MADAM: What, he's a mujra vala?

AIESHA: No, not a mujra vala like you and Ashraf ji, he's like me. He was robbed of his rusum aur ravaage [*ceremony or culture*] just like you never taught me the customs I should have had.

MADAM: He's just a very modern, educated Indian. Where's the robbery in that?

Door slams.

10lbs Marrow Bone

The shop. It's 6am. ASHRAF is setting up for opening. He brings in huge cuts of meat, putting out crates of fruit and vegetables. There is an Asian radio station playing in the background and ASHRAF is humming along to the tunes. AIESHA walks in dressed in a simple shalvar kameez suit with her headscarf wrapped in a traditional fashion as if she has been praying. She softly calls out to ASHRAF.

AIESHA: Ashraf ji… Ashraf ji… Ashr…

ASHRAF: Bloody hell girl. You scared me.

AIESHA: Sorry.

ASHRAF: What do you want?

AIESHA: Nothing.

ASHRAF: What are you doing down here; I told you I don't want you on the shop floor. (*Amuses himself.*) Well not this shop floor anyway.

AIESHA: I was…just wanted some cornflakes.

ASHRAF: They're over there. Take a box. And take some biscuits up for Madam. You know how she likes them in her tea.

AIESHA: Oh okay.

ASHRAF: I'm amazed how she never manages to lose a biscuit in her tea. She has good timing and control, just like when she used to dance.

AIESHA: Was she a good dancer?

ASHRAF: Yes she was. She would lie back on her knees and move her whole body to the nagin [*snake*] music. All the men used to watch her hips like they were hypnotising. She could have anyone one of the bastards but my darling chose me.

AIESHA: Why?

ASHRAF: What you mean why…stupid child.

AIESHA: I mean why choose you when you like boys?

ASHRAF: Shut up I don't like boys. I'm not a weirdo you know?

AIESHA: Oh? Okay. But I thought Pepsi is a boy?

ASHRAF: Are you mad, he's more a woman than you are. He's not a boy at all.

AIESHA: So what made you leave Madam?

ASHRAF: Do I look like I've left her? No, I haven't. She's my partner in life and in business. If it wasn't for her I would never have met Pepsi. Madam is a wise woman and I have lots of respect for her and so should you.

AIESHA: I do.

ASHRAF: Well show her more respect. She does more for you than any other bitch.

AIESHA: Why do you hate me?

ASHRAF: Why? You ask me why? What is there to like about you? You're always thinking about you…poor you…how the world has done wrong to you.

AIESHA: It's not the world, it's greedy…

ASHRAF: Greedy people only did what your family deserved.

AIESHA: Nobody deserves that.

ASHRAF: Just because you can read a few books it doesn't give you the right to look down your nose at people.

AIESHA: I don't.

ASHRAF: You try but you know what you are at the end of the day…a whore.

AIESHA: I hate it when you say that.

ASHRAF: That's why I say it. Until you call yourself a whore you'll never be happy.

AIESHA: Why do you hate books?

ASHRAF: Why, why, why? I hate books because I never had books; it was all the rich kids who had them. I used to see little boys go to school skipping along in their clean crisp uniforms and their packed lunches with not a care in the world. Only care they had was to make sure they knew their ABC. Their fucking ABC!

AIESHA: You know your ABC.

ASHRAF: Madam taught me and she taught me how to read and write, enough for me to get by.

AIESHA: Wow really?

ASHRAF: Just like she taught you to read the Quran. Your father was a smug book show-off. Walking through the village with his newspaper, sitting in the chai house reading the news to the waiters.

AIESHA: They liked him reading the news…

ASHRAF: I bet they would like it more if they could read their own news.

AIESHA: Anyway you didn't know him.

ASHRAF: (*Smug.*) Who says I didn't know him.

AIESHA: What?!

ASHRAF sniggers at her as if to say maybe yes.

AIESHA shakes her head as if he's just winding her up and she can't be bothered to argue about it.

AIESHA: Anyway…he could only help the best he could.

ASHRAF: Rubbish. He enjoyed having power over them. If he had any sense he'd do what Madam did for me. He'd teach them, just like he taught you more than you needed for a child of thirteen. My God you were so mouthy…

AIESHA: So you hate me because I can read.

ASHRAF: I don't hate you. You just irritate me.

AIESHA: I'm always trying to be nice to you.

ASHRAF: Exactly, you're trying to be nice when you don't actually like me.

AIESHA: I do like you.

ASHRAF: Really?

AIESHA: Yes.

ASHRAF: So you like me.

AIESHA: I always feel I'm a pain to you.

ASHRAF: You are a pain.

AIESHA: Why?

ASHRAF: Because Madam is fond of you and if Madam is fond of you then I could lose my business.

AIESHA: Why?

ASHRAF: You're not very clever for someone who can read and write in two languages, oh sorry three, I forgot the Arabic.

AIESHA: I don't really read Arabic, it's just the Quran, but I don't know what it really says.

ASHRAF: Just as well, all this religious stuff is more trouble than it's worth.

AIESHA: Is that why the men in the Masjid beat you up?

ASHRAF: That's exactly why there is so much war and hatred in the world. Religion causes it.

AIESHA: Not man?

ASHRAF: Shut up, what do you know?

AIESHA: The men in the mosques are the same men who come here at night.

ASHRAF: Well yes, some of them are.

AIESHA: No different to the men in churches and temples?

ASHRAF: And your point being?

AIESHA: The men in my books never come here. The men in my books never come to girls like me.

ASHRAF: Well the men in the books are the men who make me sick, they're also at the mosques and they're the ones that see reason and care for everyone and are clueless about the real world.

AIESHA: My abu ji [*father*] was never a religious man.

ASHRAF: Really, you could have fooled me. The way you always pray, I thought you were from some holy family.

AIESHA: No, no, abu ji always said we have to find peace in ourselves and love ourselves.

ASHRAF: Va va, what words!

AIESHA: He said religion was for those who couldn't find much to love in their lives. God will love them.

ASHRAF: So your father was a non-believer?

AIESHA: He believed, he believed in humanity.

ASHRAF: No, no, he was a non-believer. (*Laughs.*) Now I know why the bastards were after him. All this time I thought they wanted his land but instead they wanted him to pray.

AIESHA: We didn't have much land.

ASHRAF: You read books as they remind you of your father. Why do you read namaz [*pray*] five times a day? Surely your father would disapprove?

AIESHA: Like I said, if you can't find love then you look wherever, even from Namaz.

ASHRAF: You know the trouble with you, you're too clever for your own good, and you've always got an answer ready.

He moves over to her and strokes her face in a seductive way and passes his hand over her breast. Then he starts to brush her hair back away from her neck and tries to kiss her.

AIESHA feels uncomfortable and rigid.

AIESHA: Stop Ashraf. I don't like it when you do that.

ASHRAF: Yes you do like it. That's why you've come down here, when you know everyone is asleep. I told you, you're clever.

AIESHA: I came to get the cornflakes.

He forces her hand onto his groin.

I just wanted to see that the men at the mosque hadn't hurt you.

ASHRAF: Oh they hurt me but you can make it better my little book-worm.

AIESHA: Stop please.

ASHRAF: I love it when you say stop, it makes me feel you want it but are too shy to ask for it.

AIESHA: No!

PEPSI walks in panicked because he thought AIESHA was missing.

PEPSI: Oh my God, there you are... I thought I've lost Aiesha, the bitch.

ASHRAF bounces away from AIESHA and continues with his chores.

ASHRAF: The bitch is here wasting my time.

AIESHA rushes away to go back upstairs.

ASHRAF throws a dirty meat cloth at her.

Go upstairs bitch and stay there.

PEPSI: Darling don't wind yourself up. Let me calm you down. (*Feels ASHRAF has a hard on.*) Oooh, you are pleased to see me.

ASHRAF: Okay…okay…darling… Get upstairs now. I'm about to open the shop.

PEPSI kisses him passionately, ASHRAF then exits.

11lbs Oxtail Garnish

An empty blacked-out stage. Just a mirror and PEPSI's memories. PEPSI is looking in the mirror admiring himself in a very feminine manner. PEPSI is has a face mud-pack and is wearing fitted leggings and a crop vest top. He stops to think. He begins talking to himself in the mirror. Impersonating his father, a very butch and masculine character.

PEPSI: (*Holding turban fabric like a noose which he is going to use to strangle someone with.*) We're going to settle this…once and for all…you can either wear this pug on your head or round your neck. What's it going to be Ranjeet? Your neck or your head? People have got sons they're proud of but me…oh no… I had to have you…a fucking arsehole…there's only room for one of us in this house… you or me…decide bastard…decide… If you don't put this on your head then one of us is going to die. Who's it going to be?…

Bedroom at Bells. Door knocks. PEPSI composes himself and greets CHARLES. AIESHA is rubbing her hair dry with a towel. She overhears CHARLES and PEPSI talking so she quickly arranges herself on the bed, lying on her stomach reading an Oscar Wilde book. Her hair is wet and she has a towel wrapped around her. She is wearing dainty anklets.

(*Referring to the face mask.*) It's the smoke sweety.

CHARLES: Oh yes.

PEPSI: Blocks the old pores.

CHARLES: I see.

PEPSI: Did you notice my pores last night?

CHARLES: No, no.

PEPSI: Really?

CHARLES: No, didn't notice your pores.

PEPSI: Maybe it was the lights?

CHARLES: But I did notice your superb dance to Madonna.

PEPSI: Don't you just love her?

CHARLES: Yes she's super.

PEPSI: I'm still trying to get that move perfected.

CHARLES: No need Pepsi.

PEPSI: Anyway what you doing here at this time of day Charlie baby? Madam'll fuck us all over, if she finds out.

CHARLES: Actually, I brought you a little something. (*Pulls out a Madonna CD from his jacket pocket.*)

PEPSI: For me? Oh Charles, you darling.

CHARLES: Well it's just a little something.

PEPSI: It's lovely.

CHARLES: I thought you might already have them all.

PEPSI: Well I do have most of them but I don't have Madonna's *Immaculate Collection*.

CHARLES: Good.

PEPSI: Hey Juliet, Romeo's here. Thanks Charles.

PEPSI kisses CHARLES on the cheek who then has to wipe off some of PEPSI's facemask to try and make himself look nice for AIESHA.

CHARLES: It's a pleasure. I also sorted out the Masjid issue with some of the local councillors, and they were quite supportive. Surprisingly bizarre. I thought they'd be upset with me.

PEPSI: Boring, boring, boring. I hate politics, I call it bollatics.

PEPSI swipes the CD past AIESHA's nose, as if to make her jealous, joking in a childlike manner.

I've got Madonna's *Immaculate Collection*.

AIESHA: That's nice for you.

Awkward silence.

PEPSI: I'll leave you two lovebirds alone. (*He leaves.*)

CHARLES starts to kiss AIESHA from her feet to her shoulders. AIESHA carries on reading her book.

CHARLES: (*Softly trying to get her attention and seduce her away from her book.*) Aiesha, come away with me. Be mine and only mine...you're beautiful, you're perfection, you're mine. (*He holds on to her and hugs her.*) Are you mine? Or am I just feeling this way alone... Don't you feel for me what I feel for you. Could I not be Majnu and you be my Laila? You see I remembered...your Laila Majnu and I'll build you a garden just like Tom's Midnight Garden.

Pause.

Aiesha, speak to me. Come on, put your book down…this is important. I've come to ask Ashraf and Madam whether I can marry you. Well I should really get on my knees. Sorry about that. But only if you feel the same. I don't want to force you into anything.

Pause.

I know we don't know much about each other but…it'll be fine. We've got loads of time to do things together. We've got the rest of our lives. I want to know about every book you read, about what makes you smile and what makes you sad. I want to know how to be perfect for you. You've filled what has been missing in me all my life. You're my culture, my Urdu, my poetry, my history and you're my future.

CHARLES tries to kiss AIESHA on the lips.

Talk to me my love…do you love me?

AIESHA: Do I love you? Well I'm thinking to myself, do you need to ask me such a question? (*Pause.*) I want to be your happiness, I want to be your culture, I want to be your everything but I'm scared. Scared that once you've got what you're missing in your life that you won't need me anymore.

CHARLES: Never, I promise.

AIESHA: *Laila Majnu* was a tragedy, they loved and they lost.

CHARLES: Yes but remember they loved. 'Tis better to have loved and lost, than never to have loved at all'. I bet Majnu would have thought that even if Tennyson wrote it.

AIESHA: I thought it was Shakespeare.

179

CHARLES: Shakespeare, Tennyson, Oscar, who cares? All I know is they were right.

CHARLES reaches in his bag for his Oscar Wilde book. CHARLES and AIESHA lounge around.

'Some love too little, some too long,
Some sell, and others buy;
Some do the deed with many tears,
And some without a sigh;
For each man kills the thing he loves,
Yet each man does not die.'

AIESHA listens with pleasure and strokes CHARLES' brow. She finds a spot, which she starts to pick at.

(*Ruffles through the pages for an appropriate verse.*) So Oscar, my fake Eastern mysticism guide…full of eastern promise… Ouch!

AIESHA: Sorry, it was annoying me.

CHARLES: You make me feel all self-conscious.

AIESHA: Don't be silly, I'm always picking Pepsi's spots.

CHARLES: One, I'm not Pepsi and two, when I'm reading Oscar to you, it's hardly the romantic thing to do is it?

AIESHA: Well it's hardly romantic for me if I'm trying to concentrate on your exotic Wilde and you've got a spot flashing at me? (*Makes a police siren noise. He tickles her.*)

CHARLES: You cheeky little…

AIESHA: Oh, oh, stop you're tickling me!

CHARLES: Yes.

AIESHA: Stop I'm going to wet myself.

CHARLES: Yuck!!

He laughs and then just holds her. As they roll over his wallet drops out.

AIESHA hands his wallet back to him.

Thank you my love.

AIESHA: What've you got in there, it's really fat?

CHARLES: Well it's not all money for Madam.

AIESHA: I know. (*Offended.*)

CHARLES: Sorry. I didn't mean to…

AIESHA: It's okay.

CHARLES: Look, let me show you. Turn around and look.

AIESHA: It's okay.

CHARLES: I've got my family photos that I keep in here for a reminder of who I am.

AIESHA: Oh look, your mum…it is your mum isn't it?

CHARLES: Yes that's my…

AIESHA: She's wearing a sari.

CHARLES: That old lady is my mother's ayah. She must be nearly a hundred years old.

AIESHA: Wow!

CHARLES: My mum still goes to visit her in India but only at Christmas. 'Cos ayah is Christian.

AIESHA: But I thought you were Hindu?

CHARLES: No, I'm nothing really.

AIESHA: Does you mum ever wear a sari?

CHARLES: Sari? My family are more English than the English. We only speak English. I don't know hardly any Hindi. My mum's ayah only spoke English to her.

AIESHA: And so there's nothing Indian about you?

CHARLES: Yes, my heart is Indian.

AIESHA: Do you go to India?

CHARLES: Yes, I've been twice, but it was very difficult…dusty, smoky and very, very poor.

AIESHA: Mmm, I miss the smells.

CHARLES: What about the flies?

AIESHA: Yes, the flies moving busily over the fresh fruit, mangoes, mmm.

CHARLES: Do you have any pictures?

AIESHA: I have one picture. My father reading the newspaper. He's wearing his freshly ironed, starched shalvar kameez suit, sitting on the veranda next to the lemon tree. My mother in the background preparing vegetables as abu ji reads her the latest news. She's wearing a silk suit in a light mint green.

CHARLES: Can I see?

AIESHA: That is the picture, my memories.

CHARLES: Darling I'm sorry.

AIESHA: I'm sorry too.

CHARLES: Maybe one day we can go to Pakistan and India together?

AIESHA: Yes maybe.

CHARLES: You could take me to your home and family and I could find some of my family history in India.

AIESHA: I've got something to show you.

CHARLES: What's that then?

She climbs off him and gets on her hands and knees and starts searching under the bed. Eventually she rises and in her hand there is a bundle of letters all tied together with a piece of ribbon but she doesn't let go of the letters.

AIESHA: These are the letters I've written to my family. I've never posted them because I can't really remember my exact address. Or maybe it's because I know that my parents don't want to hear from me.

CHARLES: Of course they'd want to hear from you.

AIESHA: They think I'm dead.

CHARLES: Well we can prove them wrong.

AIESHA: And then what?

CHARLES: What?

AIESHA: Will they be pleased that I've turned up to shame them once again?

CHARLES: No that's not how it's going to be. They love you… I love you…do you love me, do you?

AIESHA: (*Pause.*) Yes Charles, I love you. All I do is think about you.

She sits up and straddles on him, stroking his face on every word. Kissing her way down to his waist. He moans and groans gently.

CHARLES: You're perfect.

AIESHA: 'Yet be silent, my heart! Do not count it a profitless thing
To have seen the splendour of sun, and of grass, and of flower!

To have lived and loved! For I hold that to love for an
　　hour
Is better for man and for woman than cycles of
　　blossoming spring.'

*She makes her way down towards his groin with her back to
the audience.*

*CHARLES strokes her back as he moans and groans with
pleasure but he stops her on her way down, pulls her up and
holds her.*

CHARLES: I love you.

AIESHA: Now do you believe how much I love you?

CHARLES: I promise you, we will be together forever.

AIESHA: You promise?

CHARLES: I promise. You can teach me to read Urdu so I
　　can read to you when you're old and need my eyes.

AIESHA: I think, my heart, my eyes will be more use to
　　you in our old age.

*They giggle. They rest speechless with pleasure. They caress
and fall asleep in each other's arms.*

12lbs Marinated Ribs

*Bedroom of Bells. PEPSI bursts in. Wakes up AIESHA and
CHARLES. PEPSI urges them to compose themselves as MADAM is
coming up stairs. AIESHA quickly puts on a shalvar kameez suit,
which was lying on the floor. CHARLES gets up and does his trousers
up and brushes his fingers nervously through his hair.*

PEPSI: Quick…you randy dogs…get up!

CHARLES: Oh shit! What's the time?

PEPSI: It's time you put your knob away.

AIESHA: What time is it?

PEPSI: Time you shook your booty darling.

PEPSI puts on some Asian music loud and grabs AIESHA to dance with him. They dance and CHARLES sits back and watches.

MADAM walks in.

MADAM: I see, you help us with the police and the local councillors and now you want to move in with us.

PEPSI: He was just helping with the dance.

CHARLES: I was just leaving.

MADAM: Oh, he's a choreographer now too?

CHARLES: Yes, sorry I should be going.

MADAM: You should have gone.

CHARLES: Sorry.

MADAM: Don't say sorry to me. You'll be sorry when Aieshee's out of a job.

CHARLES: Well actually… Madam…

MADAM: Yes?

CHARLES: Can I speak with you for a moment?

MADAM: What do you want now?

AIESHA looks at him longingly and in hope.

PEPSI looks a bit worried and confused.

CHARLES: In private, please.

MADAM: (*Slightly flattered.*) Oh, in private. Of course Charles. You two, haven't you got work to do? Go on, go to the other room. I'll call you when I'm done.

CHARLES gives AIESHA a gentle wave.

AIESHA and PEPSI go offstage. MADAM offers CHARLES a drink of tea from her flask.

Well Charles, do sit down.

CHARLES: Thank you.

MADAM: No, no, come over here and sit next to me.

CHARLES: Oooh… O…okay…

MADAM: Now, do have some tea with me. I get so fed up drinking it on my own.

CHARLES: Okay…thank you… (*She pours him and herself a cup.*)

MADAM: Now what was it you wanted to speak to me about in private? (*She flirts.*)

CHARLES: Well…it's tricky really.

MADAM: Don't you worry about tricks with me Charles.

CHARLES: I don't really know how to put it.

MADAM: Charles I'm older than you, a few years but I'm not senile yet. What is it you charmer you…

CHARLES: I really like you.

MADAM: Yes?

CHARLES: And Ashraf.

MADAM: Forget about him for the moment. The irritating little rat. Tell me about me? (*She strokes his thigh.*)

CHARLES: You're lovely and gracious and hospitable and…

MADAM: Yes…

CHARLES: And…and… I'm in love with Aiesha and want to pay you for her.

MADAM: What?

CHARLES: Yes… I love her and she loves me.

MADAM: No she doesn't. That's what she's paid to do!

CHARLES: No, it's different.

MADAM: You're a fool.

CHARLES: I've thought about it long and hard.

MADAM: A fool.

CHARLES: No, I'm serious. I'll pay. I'll pay you however much I can afford.

MADAM: I see your love is the sort with a price, is it?

CHARLES: No…you'll be out of pocket until she's replaced.

MADAM: Out of pocket…is that what you think… Do you ever think about how she'll cope in your world?

CHARLES: I'll treat her well and respect her.

MADAM: Are you sure Charles? Are you? She's not just a new toy for the rich boy is she?

CHARLES: You'll be replacing her soon anyway.

MADAM: Is that what you think?

CHARLES: Yes.

MADAM: Sorry… It's not the sale season at Bells. So no you can't buy Aiesha.

CHARLES: I don't mean to buy her. I was just trying to cover your loss of profits until you replace her.

MADAM: What happens when you want to replace her? Where does she go then?

CHARLES: I won't want to.

MADAM: Well you seem to have the money for it.

CHARLES: It's not the money. I don't care about the money…she makes me feel real. The money is just my savings.

MADAM: That's our profession Charles. I can make you feel real. Even Pepsi can. And heaven knows Ashraf would probably manage it too.

CHARLES: We think alike. We read the same things. She believes in me and I believe in her. She needs looking after.

MADAM: Have you thought what she might mean to us?

CHARLES: You're going to be sending her back to Lahore in a month or so…

MADAM: Lahore? So she's told you about Heera Mandi. I've never had children Charles. But Aieshee she kept me going, reading her little fantasy stories to me. Cuddling up to me in the night when she was scared. I love her too.

CHARLES: Well you'll want the best for her?

MADAM: Yes I do and the best for her in our whore-ish world is to stick together. We can fight the world together but alone we'll wither and die.

CHARLES: I'll treat her like a princess.

MADAM: What, you'll have her cooking and cleaning for you and trapped in a house where she only meets your select friends who'll try to rape her when you're not around.

CHARLES: My friends aren't like that and my family will be very welcoming to her.

MADAM: Oh yes, your family?

CHARLES: Yes my family knows about her.

MADAM: Really Charles? And they're proud that their son is bringing a whore for a daughter-in-law.

CHARLES: When she's with me she won't be a whore, she'll be my wife.

MADAM: I suppose you've checked out the immigration legalities?

CHARLES: Yes I'm waiting for a solicitor friend of mine to get back to me. But even if it means we have to go back to Pakistan for while, I've got…

MADAM: Go back to Pakistan? You really are stupid. She'll get killed out there. We live in protected communities and outside of that you're on your own and God help you if anyone knows what either of you have done.

CHARLES: Let's not argue. I've got twenty thousand saved and I can get it to you by the morning.

MADAM: Twenty thousand pounds…is that the price of love?

CHARLES: No, but it's what I can get to you in cash by the morning.

MADAM: I don't want to argue. Let me just say this to you once and I want you to listen clearly. Aieshee is not for permanent sale. You can hire her for a few hours but then she's with us. We love her and know her. You don't. Don't ever come to me again with such a ridiculous offer.

Don't try to be clever and mention it to Ashraf as he'll take your money and not give you Aieshee. He'll just send her back on the first flight to Pakistan… Think very clearly Charles. You don't want that for Aieshee, do you?

CHARLES: But Madam she's a girl with hopes and aspirations. You can't keep her like this. (*His eyes start to fill with tears.*)

MADAM: I know what I can and can't do.

CHARLES: I can't carry on without her.

MADAM: You will. Believe me you will.

CHARLES: I want to be with her all the time.

MADAM: Grow up, you can't even if she was living with you. You have to work and…stop playing the fool. You just carry on coming here in the evenings. Make your love come true. I bet most of your love is lost in your trousers. Because if it was in your heart, you'd be behaving more sensibly.

CHARLES: Haven't you ever wanted to settle down with the man you love?

MADAM: Yes I have. It's called love with compromise. That's what you'll have to do

CHARLES: How are we to compromise? (*Pause.*)

MADAM: Like I've had to. (*Pause.*) I loved Ashraf. I left everything for him. I didn't listen to my madam. She told me I'd feel pain. She said: 'In love there are no boundaries to keep you sane. Out of love reality always hits you on the head each morning.' Well I got hit on the head by Ashraf. We came to this country and life was never the same again.

CHARLES: That's really horrible, I'm sorry…

MADAM: Shut up Charles. It's not horrible, it's reality. Keep your mouth shut and stop feeding Aiesha with foolish ideas or I'll stop you from seeing her.

CHARLES: I'm really sorry for your pain but I'm hurting too. Aiesha and I are different from you people and I *will* look after her. I *will*.

He cries and sobs as he leaves.

MADAM watches him break down and wants to console him but holds back.

13lbs Intestine

A melodic Islamic call for prayer plays on the broken decorative Azan clock.

ASHRAF, MADAM and AIESHA are all occupied reading Namaz. They're at various stages of either having read Namaz or folding up their prayer mats, to being completely absorbed in prayer. Everyone is silent. There is some slight interaction between characters when they're not reading Namaz but this is just merely to pass a book to each other or to shove up on the sofa.

Both AIESHA and MADAM have their heads covered with their dupatta and ASHRAF is wearing a prayer hat. The three finish Namaz and fold up their mats.

In the background PEPSI is looking in the mirror admiring himself in a very feminine manner. He stops to think. PEPSI begins talking to himself in the mirror. Impersonating his mother.

PEPSI: So you think you've made it in the big world. You've picked a nackli musliman [*fake Muslim*] to be your father. Instead of a paag [*turban*] what's he making you wear? Was it all worth it my precious boy, tell me is it all worth it?… What have I been left with, your pictures, your memories, your pain…your father? What have I been left with?

As AIESHA is finishing off her prayers she notices PEPSI in front of the mirror. She leaves her prayer mat and goes over to him. PEPSI is swaying back and forth.

AIESHA holds him close and kisses his forehead.

PEPSI holds onto AIESHA tightly and begins to cry.

Don't leave me, don't leave me? Everyone leaves me.

AIESHA: Shhh. shhhh…it's okay…shhh.

14lbs Sheep's Trotters

There are three see-through curtains with strong lighting behind them. The audience can see silhouettes, of the cast. Behind each curtain there are couples having sex at Bells. On the left-hand side ASHRAF is buggering PEPSI. In the middle is AIESHA and CHARLES. On the right hand side is MADAM, wearing her shalvar kameez and dupatta on her head, with a naked CUSTOMER tied up on a crucifix. She's playing the dominatrix with a whip. The background music is the style of a classical Islamic tune by Nusrat Fateh Ali Khan which is like a Sufi chant.

ASHRAF: Who's the daddy? Have you been a bad girl today?

PEPSI: Yes very bad.

ASHRAF: I'm going to have to punish you.

PEPSI: What's my punishment?

ASHRAF: It's bad, it's really bad.

PEPSI: What is it? Tell me please?

ASHRAF: How sorry are you?

PEPSI: I'm not sorry at all.

ASHRAF: Well then my bitch you're going to suffer, turn around and suck…

MADAM: Why did you wet yourself last night?

CUSTOMER 2: I'm sorry mum I don't know.

MADAM: I've had to wash that bed every day this week.

CUSTOMER 2: Sorry mum.

MADAM: My hands are red raw. Sore from scrubbing your bed.

AIESHA and CHARLES lying on the bed holding each other. AIESHA climbs off him and gets on her hands and knees and starts searching under the bed. Eventually she rises and in her hand there is a bundle of letters all tied together with a piece of ribbon.

CHARLES: You're beautiful, a princess.

AIESHA: Abu ji called me his princess.

CHARLES: Abu ji still does.

AIESHA: Look?

CHARLES: Tons more letters here. Do you ever read them back to yourself?

AIESHA: No never.

They go quiet and she sits and stares at CHARLES whilst he goes through the letters. Every now and then he looks up at her and smiles. He hugs her and they lay back and she reads a letter to him.

AIESHA: My darling abu ji. Us salam oliekum. I hope this letter reaches you in good health and fortune. I'm sorry I haven't written for so long but it's been busy here. (*To CHARLES.*) I had to lie. (*Then back to reading her letter.*) I'm training to be a nurse. I've been learning how to look after people when they are sick, sick in the head. Mental illness. I'm at a good nursing school in London, the school of Bells, and I hope my studies will finish for the summer and I can visit you...

CHARLES: Oh fuck it...fuck it...fuck it...put them in a bag and let's just go, let's get out of here now. What's there to stop us? Life's too bloody short.

AIESHA: What now...really now? (*She jumps up and grabs the nearest bag and stuffs a few things in it.*)

CHARLES: Yes now.

Back in MADAM's room.

CUSTOMER 2: I won't do it again mum.

MADAM: No you won't because I'm going to rub your little willie in it, till it's raw like my hands.

CUSTOMER 2: No, please, don't hurt me.

MADAM: You won't be able to pee from it then will you?

CUSTOMER 2: Oh mum I won't do it again.

MADAM: Will you? I didn't hear you, you wimp.

CUSTOMER 2: No, sorry mum.

CHARLES and AIESHA start to creep out of the room. CHARLES is holding onto AIESHA to protect her. They try various windows and doors; they struggle with the exit door. As they get to the exit door AIESHA's bag knocks over madam's flask, which was on a table. They stumble around in the dark. The noise disturbs everyone.

ASHRAF runs out tying up his sarong [dhoti] and PEPSI runs out tying his dressing gown, which is an elegant silk floral number.

MADAM also rushes out with her whip in her hand, leaving her CUSTOMER whimpering.

PEPSI is slightly hysterical and panicking.

MADAM is calm but ASHRAF is angry.

Background whimpering noises from the CUSTOMER.

PEPSI: Oh my god oh my god! Aiesha what you doing, silly girl.

ASHRAF: You bastard Charles!

PEPSI: What you doing? For fuck's sake. Let her go.

AIESHA starts to cry.

CHARLES: We love each other.

ASHRAF: What? You love…

PEPSI: For fuck's sake. You twat…

ASHRAF: Aiesha come back here at once. I'm going to fucking kill you.

PEPSI: Aiesha just get back here will you please.

CHARLES: No she's going with me. (*Holding on to her.*)

ASHRAF: You bastard you come into my house and backchat me? Let her go.

CHARLES: No!

AIESHA: (*Calmly sobbing and pleading.*) Madam…please… Madam… I beg you please…let me go…please?

ASHRAF grabs AIESHA but CHARLES holds onto to her and she holds onto CHARLES. ASHRAF attacks both CHARLES and AIESHA.

CHARLES: Ashraf…stop it…for fuck's sake…get off you idiot…let's sort it out like gentlemen.

AIESHA: Get off…you're hurting me… Madam…please… Pepsi…help me.

PEPSI: You said you wouldn't leave me.

MADAM: Leave it Ashraf, leave them.

ASHRAF: I can't believe this girl.

MADAM: I said leave them.

All of a sudden MADAM whips ASHRAF and he falls to the ground.

PEPSI goes to ASHRAF all worried and concerned.

PEPSI: My baby… Ash darling, are you okay?

ASHRAF: What the bloody hell you doing woman?

PEPSI: Yeah Madam it's that cocktail Indian bastard you're supposed to be aiming at, not my baby.

ASHRAF: You gone mad? Paagal kooti! [*Mad dog!*]

She whips ASHRAF again but misses purposely.

PEPSI starts howling and whimpering.

MADAM: Shut up you hysterical clown.

She throws the keys at CHARLES who catches them. He fumbles around, trying to unlock the door.

Okay Charles have it your way. But remember this is not the end. You take Aieshee but let me tell you if I ever see or hear from you again you won't know what evil I can cause.

ASHRAF: (*Confused.*) You what…What you… What are you saying?

She whips both ASHRAF and PEPSI with one lash.

MADAM: Go on get out. Get out the pair of you!

They rush out as fast as they can.

AIESHA: I love you Madam.

At hearing AIESHA call out 'I love you' MADAM's aggressive exterior melts with a sigh and she breaks down and cries.

Exit music plays: 'Sajjana ne phul mariya' ['My sweetheart has hit me with flowers'].

MADAM: I love you too.

ASHRAF: You fucking stupid bitch.

ASHRAF charges towards her and slaps her to the ground. MADAM starts to cry.

PEPSI can't handle seeing the violence and crouches in a corner, shaking and hiding his face from ASHRAF beating MADAM.

The End